BACK BAY

A LIVING PORTRAIT

BACK BAY

A LIVING PORTRAIT

Barbara W. Moore and Gail Weesner

INTERIOR PHOTOGRAPHS BY SOUTHIE BURGIN

EXTERIOR PHOTOGRAPHS BY BARBARA W. MOORE

ILLUSTRATIONS BY CONSTANCE SCHNITGER

CENTRY HILL PRESS
Boston, Massachusetts

DESIGNER: *Dede Cummings*

COPY EDITOR: *Anne Swanson*

PRINTER: *South China Printing Company Limited, Hong Kong*

Endpapers: The scene on the endpapers presents "Boston from Parker Hill," a watercolor by Edwin Whitefield, 1866, from a private collection. A detail of a panoramic view from the southwest, it shows Back Bay, the Mill Dam and Cross Dam, and the railroad tracks over the flats. Most of the houses on Arlington Street appear to be finished.

Published in 1995 by Centry Hill Press, Box 306, Charles Street Station, Boston, Massachusetts 02114

Library of Congress Catalog Card Number 95-67827

ISBN 0-9632077-2-5 (cloth)
        0-9632077-3-3 (paper)

ACKNOWLEDGMENTS

The authors wish to thank the following individuals for advice, cooperation, and assistance in preparing this book: Maria Aronson, Jacob M. Atwood, Dr. and Mrs. W. Gerald Austen, Smoki Bacon, Ron Berkowitz, Sally Brewster, Nancy Brickley, Mr. and Mrs. V. B. Castellani, Ralph and Susan Cole, William E. Crawford, Robert and Judy Del Col, Catharine-Mary Donovan, Joan W. Eldredge, Dr. and Mrs. Anthony C. Erdmann, J. Brent and Karen Finnegan, Cynthia Fleming, Anne Harney and Herb Gallagher, Lois R. Kunian, Vicki Harris Lemberg, Cecile Lemley, Harriet and Alan Lewis, The Rev. and Mrs. Samuel T. Lloyd III, Connie Marchiel, Sally McGinty, Margo Miller, William B. and Nancy Osgood, The Rev. Barbara H. Nielsen, Joseph H. Palermino, Susan Park, Margaret and Gene Pokorny, John Sears, Catherine L. Seiberling, Anne Sullivan, Thomas Sweeney III, Stella M. Trafford, Nancy Tye, Marian Ullman, Mr. and Mrs. Peter S. Voss.

We also gratefully acknowledge the invaluable assistance of the following: William Young at the Back Bay Architectural Commission, Sally Pierce and Catharina Slautterback at the Boston Athenaeum, The Boston Center for Adult Education, Sinclair Hitchings and Aaron Schmidt at the Boston Public Library, Boston University Women's Council, Philip Bergen and Dan McCormick at the Bostonian Society, Burrage House, Jill McArthur at Childs, Bertman, Tseckares, Inc., the Commonwealth School, Bob Fleming at Emerson College, Fisher College, Phebe Goodman at Friends of Copley Square, Edward W. Gordon at the Gibson House Museum, Goethe-Institut Boston, Halcyon Place, Hale House, the principal and families of the Kingsley Montessori School, Chris Steele at the Massachusetts Historical Society, Kimberly Alexander Shilland at Massachusetts Institute of Technology, Maureen Melton at the Museum of Fine Arts, Anne Clifford and Lorna Conlon at the Society for the Preservation of New England Antiquities, Elaine Anderson at the Neighborhood Association of the Back Bay, the New England School of Optometry, and The Raymond Cattle Company.

Finally, our special thanks to Stuart Drake and Ken MacRae for sharing their knowledge of and enthusiasm for the neighborhood by reading the manuscript and offering their encouragement and advice, and to our friend Anne Swanson, whom we persuaded to be our copy editor, but who has contributed so much more.

INTRODUCTION

THREE YEARS AGO we produced and published a book about our own Boston neighborhood, Beacon Hill. To prepare that volume, we took a closer look at the streets we knew so well, and we entered our neighbors' homes to photograph their interiors. The experience was rewarding, so we considered writing a companion volume about a second Boston neighborhood. Back Bay was the logical choice — developed soon after Beacon Hill, it adjoins its older neighbor. In addition, the two have much in common: They share the same elected representatives at the local, state, and federal levels, and both are historic and architectural treasures.

But Back Bay presented a greater challenge than Beacon Hill: The land area is much greater, the architecture is more diverse, and the wrecking ball has destroyed more of the earlier fabric. In addition, this was not our home territory, but new ground. We were amazed to discover the overwhelming warmth, generosity, hospitality, and genuine interest we met at every turn. Individual residents as well as institutions opened their doors, allowing us to photograph the wonderful interiors seen on these pages. We were given invaluable information, sometimes physical help in moving heavy furniture, and even an invitation to a shared meal with newfound friends. We feel confident that this book includes a very fine sampling of Back Bay interiors, which we could never have obtained without the cooperation of the people who live in the district.

In matters of architectural history, we had a precious resource in the work of the late Bainbridge Bunting, whose 1952 Ph.D. thesis was developed into the remarkable book, *Houses of the Bay Bay* (Harvard University Press, 1967). Bunting's research was generally flawless, and we have accepted his attributions and dates unless there is a strong argument to the contrary. We have also relied heavily on his interpretations of architectural styles and periods, and on his superb historical survey of the development of the Back Bay district. In short, our debt to Bunting is immeasurable.

Despite Bunting's deep understanding and appreciation of the district, one sometimes senses a note of concern, if not distress, about the future. Between the lines, Bunting implies a certain pessimism about Back Bay, its streets "stifled with parked cars and local traffic," surrounded by the "heightening silhouettes of modern apartment buildings on the area's periphery." More specifically, Bunting warns that "the challenge which confronts us now is whether we can forestall the attempt of a few property owners to pull down the present structures and erect new and bigger ones which will destroy the domestic scale and architectural continuity of the district — forestall them long enough for Boston's citizens to awake to the unique architectural importance of the Back Bay district." Thirty years later some of Bunting's concerns remain, but a new awakening has fostered some semblance of control. A protected architectural district under the watchful eye of vigilant local groups, the Neighborhood Association of the Back Bay and the Back Bay Association of businesses, the district has the handsome good looks and self-confident bearing of a survivor.

NOTE: One of our earliest and most difficult decisions was to define the western limit of the Back Bay neighborhood. Friends and advisors urged us to include Kenmore Square and the Fenway — or Charlesgate at the very least — and it was with great reluctance that we ultimately drew the line at Massachusetts Avenue. In the end, the decision was simply one of economy — economy of space, as our projected 120 pages had already increased to 144. Thus we established our boundary near the line of the old Cross Dam, leaving Gravelly Point and the Full Basin for a later project.

CONTENTS

THE GREAT BAY
A Pictorial History of Back Bay

REVIEWING THE HISTORY of the Boston residential neighborhood known as Back Bay, one is struck with how frequently the tale is told in superlatives. The *greatest,* the *finest,* the *most remarkable* — the theme recurs across more than three centuries and persists to the present day.

Even its earliest name was extravagant: In a small peninsular town studded with coves, bays, and inlets, this spreading swampland was distinguished as The Great Bay. An estuary of the Charles River (see map below), its tidal flats spread across some 450 marshy acres on the south side of the river, with about as large a tract across the river in Cambridge. Eventually,

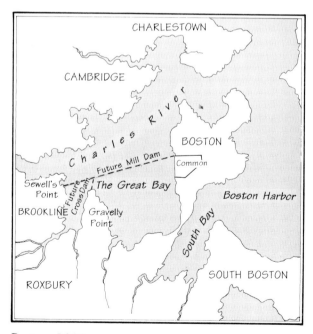

Boston, 1800

because the bay was nestled behind the original Boston peninsula, it became known as the "back" bay.

By all accounts it was a pleasant place, from which the colonists liked to watch the sunset from the foot of the Common, the haunt of duck hunters, fishermen, and "mudlarking boys." A later reminiscence recalls "a beautiful sheet of water, spreading out from the city, with the Brookline hills rising beyond."

For a brief historical moment the bay was actually center stage: In April 1775, English troops embarked across Back Bay waters for fateful encounters at Lexington and Concord. Except for this single incident, however, the marshes remained an anonymous expanse, receiving little attention until the second decade of the nineteenth century.

During those sleepy years, there was some limited filling of the low-lying shoreline as private property owners claimed riparian rights to the land above the low-water mark. This matter of riparian ownership would become an important issue around 1850, when the entire bay assumed a value beyond the wildest dreams of earlier generations.

MILL DAM

The narrative now moves to June 1813, when a Boston town meeting heard a bold new proposal. An enterprising group calling themselves the Boston and Roxbury Mill Corporation petitioned the town "for liberty to build a Mill Dam and Turnpike Road from the bottom of Beacon Street" westward across the bay to a Brookline promontory known as Sewell's Point, about a mile and a half distant.

The proposal was actually part of a much larger scheme (never executed) to construct a network of canals, dams, and basins encircling the Boston peninsula from Roxbury to Brookline to Cambridge to Charlestown. The leading figure among the promoters was Uriah Cotting, well known as a skilled engineer and shrewd businessman who had spearheaded massive improvements along Boston's waterfront a decade earlier. In his day Cotting was respected as a man "of great genius and industry" and of "a sober judgment."

In this case, Cotting's judgment (and also his luck) would fail him. Construction of the dam proved slow and expensive; the project stalled, ran short of funds, and was not begun in earnest for five years. Cotting himself died before the dam was finished. But in the early morning hours of July 2, 1821, the Mill Dam was finally opened to traffic with a modest ceremony in which a small cavalcade crossing over the dam from Brookline was welcomed by a delegation of waiting Bostonians.

The new dam was basically a massive dike. Fifty feet wide and a mile and a half long, it was faced with stone from a local quarry. A gravel toll road ran along the river side of the causeway, and on the bay side was a plank walk planted with poplars. About midway to the Brookline shore, near today's Dartmouth Street, stood a tollhouse. Nearby for a time was a mill for grinding corn and then, in the vicinity of Massachusetts Avenue, a short cross dam

that ran south to Gravelly Point in Roxbury, dividing the bay in two (see map below). At high tide water passed through floodgates into the so-called Full Basin, located behind Gravelly Point. At the mill sites the water moved through sluices, generating power as it passed into the Receiving Basin, from which it drained back into the Charles River through gates in the main dam.

The mills at Gravelly Point were only a qualified success. Apparently the generating power of the Back Bay tides did not live up to expectations. Moreover, railroad tracks built over the flats (below) and continued filling of the shoreline by private owners further impeded the tidal flow. In the end, however, the

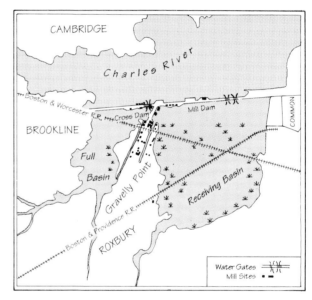

The Great Bay, 1850

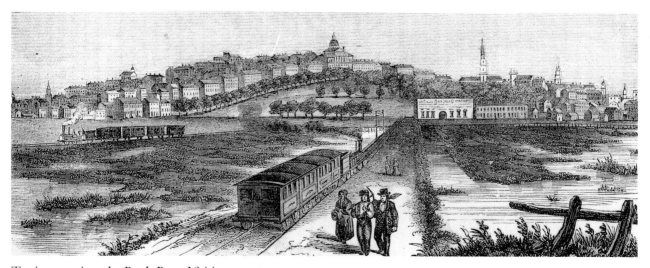

Trains crossing the Back Bay, 1844

water-power project failed because it was based on an obsolescent technology. The dominant force of the age would be the steam engine, which, powering mechanical shovels and locomotives, would transform this soggy marshland into terra firma.

From a modern perspective, the lasting importance of the Mill Dam was as a thoroughfare. Renamed Western Avenue, then later Beacon Street, the causeway provided a direct route westward to the mainland in Brookline. Symbolically as well as physically, this link effectively ended Boston's peninsular existence. For some thirty years, however, it was a working mill dam. Its image survives in the two renderings reproduced here. Colonel Head was a Canadian who apparently sketched the scene when visiting Boston in 1847. Vautin was a professional artist who in 1860 had worked in the city for more than twenty years. Both views are perplexing, especially Vautin's, with its odd perspective and scattering of sheds and shanties. Perhaps it was a nostalgic rendering — more romance than reality.

There is indeed a romance about the place. Entombed beneath the pavement of modern Beacon Street, the old roadway still evokes some vividly haunting scenes: The straight, broad sweep was a natural racetrack. There are images of winter sleighrides across the frozen waters, and a lively account of visiting celebrity Charles Dickens and his friend "Jamie" Fields trekking the Mill Dam one February morning, "puffing like two steam engines" and reciting lines from Dickens's works.

Most haunting, perhaps, is the photograph seen on the opposite page. Dating from the

The Mill Dam, 1847,
by Lieutenant Colonel George Edward Head

mid-1850s, it is a view from the State House dome. Dominating the scene, the Mill Dam bravely spans the Back Bay wasteland. Here one can sense the boldness of the vision of the men who planned it. In the middle distance is the ghostly outline of the "City Mills" on the cross dam, following the line of modern Hemenway Street, and faint images of the tollhouse, a few shanties, and a mysterious hotel that appeared for several years upon the main causeway. Within a decade this scene — and soon all memory of it — would vanish.

THE RAILROADS

By 1835, two pairs of rail tracks crossed the Back Bay mud, forming a giant "X" as they intersected just south of today's Copley Square. From northwest to southeast ran the Boston and Worcester line, later known as the Boston

The Mill Dam, 1860, by N. Vautin

Looking west from the State House, 1858

and Albany; from southwest to northeast cut the Boston and Providence to its terminal at Park Square. These routes left a permanent imprint on the map of the city, forming the boundary between the South End and Back Bay and determining the site and shape of such landmarks as Copley and Kenmore squares, the Massachusetts Turnpike and the Amtrak lines, and Back Bay Station.

Time and again the Back Bay story interweaves with that of the railroads. By impeding the tidal flow, the rail lines undermined the efficiency of the Mill Dam and contributed to the increasing pollution of the Receiving Basin. The tracks of the Worcester line would permanently define the southern boundary of the Back Bay residential district, confining it and dividing it from the city-sponsored development taking place in the South End. The two neighborhoods were never successfully merged. Before the creation of the Prudential Center in the late 1950s, grim railroad yards sprawled across acres of valuable Back Bay land, further isolating the South End.

On the other hand, it was rail technology that created the Back Bay district. Without the tracks, the steam locomotive, and steam-powered shovels, the Back Bay project would have been impossible. Moreover, the Age of Steam would transform Boston from a harbor-bound provincial town into a modern city, the regional hub of the fast-growing national rail network. Locally the new

technology made fortunes, and many a Back Bay mansion was erected with wealth derived from the twin technologies of rail and steam.

BACK BAY NUISANCE

From the outset the Receiving Basin was a source of trouble. First it was dust: "When the water was shut off from the Back Bay [in 1820], the dirt became dry, and many persons . . . can well remember the clouds of fine dust . . . which took possession of every crevice of their houses." This complaint was settled by adding an extra sluice in the main dam, but other problems soon developed.

Because the Mill Dam had cut off the cleansing flow of the tides, the shallow waters became stagnant. The situation was exacerbated by the rail causeways and by private landfill projects along the fringes of the bay. But the real crisis probably dates from 1827, when Boston obtained the right to discharge sewage into the Receiving Basin. For two decades the city's waste poured into the shallow, landlocked bay, and by midcentury the Back Bay was an unqualified environmental disaster.

On this theme, Bostonians of the day displayed an enviable descriptive talent: "the abode of filth and disease" from which "every western wind sends its pestilential exhalations across the entire city" . . . "mournful and odorous" . . . "nothing less than a great cesspool." While the public ranted, the board of health declared that something must be done. In 1849 the bay was declared a nuisance, and a commission was named to review the issue. Three years later the verdict was delivered: The Back Bay was unhealthy and unsightly, and the commissioners recommended filling the entire area with clean gravel, providing it with proper drainage, and laying it out in "wide and ample roads." A new commission was then created "to devise a plan for laying out and filling the new lands."

GROWING PAINS

While the plan was bold, the concept was far from new. Bostonians had been making land since the earliest years, and by 1850 they had increased the size of the original land mass by more than fifty percent. By this date, however, the snug peninsula was again filled to capacity.

At first the city turned to a plan dating from 1801, probably the design of Charles Bulfinch, which called for filling the mud flats adjacent to Boston Neck. This was the beginning of the modern South End, which was filled and developed in a northerly direction until it finally connected with the Commonwealth's Back Bay lands around 1870 (see map). In the mode of London, the South End took the form of a series of housing developments centered upon small green squares. Blackstone and Franklin squares were built in 1849, Chester Square in 1850, and Worcester and Union a year later. Linking the squares were broad, European-style avenues, typically lined with long, uniform rows of houses like those seen below.

Much has been made of the differences between the "English" South End and the

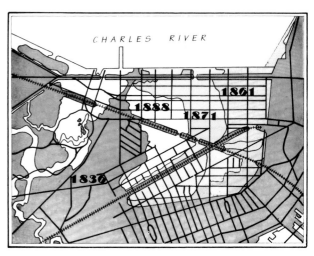

Back Bay and the South End

"French" Back Bay. Nonetheless, the two developments had much in common. Plans for both of these government-sponsored projects were adopted at about the same time — the city approved its South End plan in 1850, and the Commonwealth's Back Bay scheme was essentially complete by 1855. Both were built on broad new acres of filled land, allowing Bostonians to indulge in an entirely new approach to city planning. The major streets in both districts were plotted on a generous scale with the long vistas so admired in European cities of the day. Height and setback restrictions assured a dignified, unified streetscape, and a system of alleyways routed household services to the rear of the dwellings. Neither neighborhood as planned provided a commercial district for local shops.

To this extent the rival developments were conceptually similar. In terms of architectural vision, however, they were strikingly different.

South End houses by N. J. Bradlee

The Public Garden, 1857

The typical South End dwelling was traditional and conservative — a high-stooped version of the Beacon Hill bowfront embellished with Italianate details and capped with a French-style mansard roof. This model was no match for the sleek, continental-style brownstone blocks that soon rose in Back Bay. The South End became old-fashioned and stodgy almost overnight, and like the father of John P. Marquand's George Apley, status-conscious South Enders removed themselves to the chic new district.

Another important nineteenth-century landfill created today's Public Garden. The Back Bay flats once extended eastward to the line of present-day Charles Street, where early filling was probably considered an extension of the Common. For several decades the shoreline was used for ropemaking, a messy and very flammable business that properly belonged at the edge of town. By 1837, however, this area was no longer remote. Boston was now a city (incorporated in 1822); the building of Beacon Hill was almost complete, cows no longer grazed on the Common, and the Mill Dam had become a fashionable place for promenading. The year was marked by a private effort to create a botanical garden. A group of men calling themselves the Proprietors of the Public Garden leased the old ropewalk site and did a little more filling. For about a decade they operated the Garden as a private enterprise, charging admission to view the various horticultural exhibits installed there, including such popular attractions as "a complete bed of prize tulips," the first such display in America.

From this era we have a photo (above) showing Ralph Waldo Emerson and Oliver Wendell Holmes seated near a greenhouse that once stood near Beacon Street. Beyond this image, information about the early Public Garden is scant, but its condition so declined that by midcentury it was an eyesore and a dumping ground, its future soon tied to that of the wretched Back Bay flats.

In the end, of course, the Garden did flower. In 1856, Boston was offered about three acres of mud flats in return for a promise to preserve the Garden forever "for horticultural purposes." Tempted by potential revenue, the city resisted this proposal for several years, but in 1859 sprang into action by announcing a competition for a suitable design for the new Public Garden.

The prizewinning plan (below) was the work of a young architect named George F. Meacham. While its details have been altered, its major features are recognizable: meandering paths with statues and fountains, and an artificial pond with a gently curving shoreline.

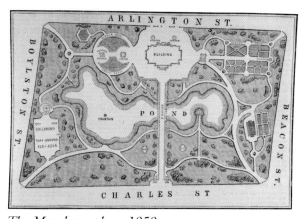

The Meacham plan, 1859

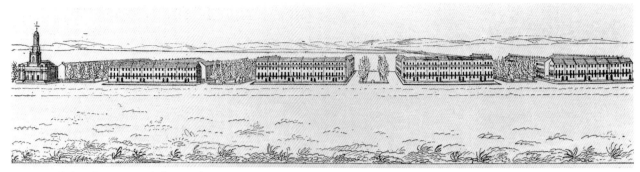

Proposed development of the Back Bay, 1824

(The proposed building was a new city hall, which was subsequently built on School Street.) Though this is the only known landscape plan of Meacham's career, he later designed several buildings in the Back Bay district (page 21).

With a plan in hand, work progressed rapidly, and as the first new houses rose on Arlington Street, the Public Garden also began to take form. The city would later be criticized for its uncooperative behavior during the Back Bay negotiations. To its credit, however, it gave to the state's Back Bay project an enchanting front yard.

EARLY SCHEMES

In 1844 a visiting Scotsman named Robert Fleming Gourlay looked across the brackish Back Bay shallows and pronounced them "the finest site in the world for a new town." Gourlay was not the first man of vision to reach this conclusion. In fact, speculators had been eyeing these mud flats for decades.

It was, of course, an obvious solution. The peninsula was overcrowded, and the city had no other direction in which to expand. As Boston entered an era of lusty economic growth, the older residential neighborhoods fell to commercial interests, leaving only Beacon Hill as a desirable area for the growing numbers of prosperous citizens. It was in this context that Bostonians turned their attention to the maligned, polluted Back Bay flats.

One of the most intriguing sidelights in this chronicle concerns a small aquatint that appeared in an 1825 edition of *A History of Boston* by Dr. Caleb H. Snow. Reproduced above, it presents a strikingly prophetic rendition of the Back Bay plan — published only four years after completion of the Mill Dam and some 35 years before the filling

project actually began! Where did it come from and where did it languish before re-emerging more than three decades later?

During those years some half-dozen other schemes were put forward. Two of the most fanciful are seen here. Gourlay's 1844 plan featured a kidney-shaped waterway sweeping across most of today's Back Bay and South End,

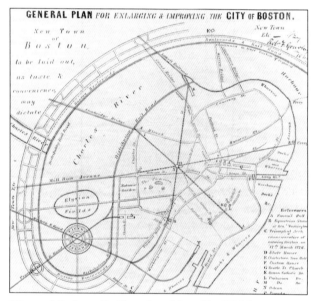

Plan of Robert F. Gourlay (detail), 1844

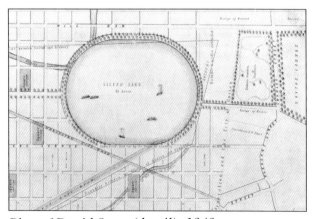

Plan of David Sears (detail), 1849

adorned with two artificial islands and encircled by "boulevards" constructed atop an underground rail system. A somewhat later scheme was proposed by prominent Bostonian (and mud flat investor) David Sears. This plan envisioned several London-style squares and a 75-acre lake over much of the modern residential district.

SOLUTIONS

In the meantime the City of Boston, the Commonwealth of Massachusetts, and various private and commercial landowners haggled over land rights. It was a great tangle of conflicting interests, further complicated because parts of the flats lay within the towns of Brookline and Roxbury. Moreover, the City of Boston was uncooperative throughout the negotiating process, claiming ownership to lands to which it had no rights at all, and then obstructing efforts to coordinate the pattern of Back Bay streets with those in the South End.

The affair dragged on until 1856, when most of the claims were settled in a document known as the Tripartite Agreement. Signed by the city, the state, and the successors to Uriah Cotting's old mill corporation, the agreement was based on a 1641 ordinance. It gave the state clear title to a parcel of approximately 100 acres, embracing most of today's residential district westward to a meandering line between Exeter and Fairfield streets. All lands west of this line, as well as the water side of Beacon Street, were awarded to the old mill corporation — now a

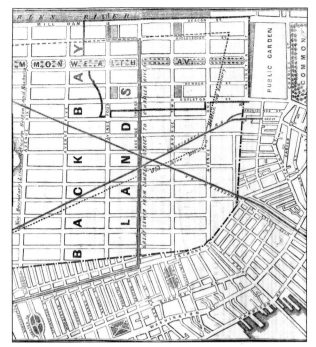

Plan for Back Bay lands, 1858

land company with a very bright future. The city, receiving only a scant few acres at the foot of the Public Garden, might appear the loser. However, since the boundaries of both Brookline and Roxbury were redrawn to place the entire bay within the territorial limits of Boston, the city's long-term gains were in fact enormous.

The map reproduced on this page appeared in the April 23, 1858, *Saturday Evening Gazette*. It is one in a series of maps and plans that document the evolution of the Back Bay

Westbourne Terrace, Hyde Park, London, circa 1855

venture throughout the 1850s. As in the anonymous 1825 plan, the district took the form of a simple grid with the major streets running east to west, parallel to the Mill Dam. The streets were long and broad, and the dominant axis (Commonwealth Avenue) featured a central tree-lined mall. The plan presents a fairly accurate outline of the Back Bay neighborhood today. To the south, however, it carries the grid across the railroad tracks, where it collides awkwardly with the South End streets. The problem of this junction, though eventually modified, exists to the present day.

To ensure an open, spacious scale, the state allotted a generous 43 percent of the total filled area for streets and parks; another 8 percent would be donated to schools, museums, and other public institutions. Deed restrictions controlled the height and setbacks of all houses constructed along the new streets: buildings must be at least three stories high; there would be no frame buildings, and private stables were restricted. Household services would be delivered via a system of alleyways. Commercial establishments were limited and manufacturing activities were banned from the entire district. Scattered across the area were three small parks, of which only one, Copley Square, was ever built.

These were the key features of the street system that had begun to emerge around 1855 under the sponsorship of architect Arthur Gilman. Gilman had just returned from Europe, having spent several months both in London and in Paris. During that time, the French capital was being rebuilt by Napoleon III's préfet of the Seine, Baron Georges-Eugène Haussmann, and it is sometimes said that Second Empire Paris provided the inspiration for Gilman's Back Bay design.

In fact, however, Gilman arrived in Paris in the spring of 1853, when massive demolitions were well underway, but far too early to witness the splendors of Haussmann's grand boulevards. He would have seen some of the earlier improvements such as Louis XV's Champs Elysées or the 1850 rue de Rivoli. But in England he must have viewed some of London's new urban developments, like Westbourne Terrace, which rose in Hyde Park between 1850 and 1855. Indeed, the view of this district on page 15 seems as likely a model for Gilman's Back Bay as any Parisian boulevard.

THE GREAT FILL

It was an enormous project — the largest in the world, they said at the time. Eyewitness accounts describe a round-the-clock operation of stupendous proportions, unthinkable even a generation earlier.

Fewer than fifty years separate the two pictures on this page. The view on the left, based on an 1811 drawing, shows the operation by which the heirs of John Hancock cut 60 feet from the top of Beacon Hill, which they then sold as fill for the nearby Mill Pond. Though there are no precise records of this earthmoving, there are very good ones from the year 1835, when neighboring Pemberton Hill

Excavation of Beacon Hill, 1811

Excavation in Needham, circa 1860

Arlington Street Church, 1862

Museum of Natural History, circa 1864

was also lowered. The contractor for this project, a Wilmington farmer named Asa Sheldon, moved 100,000 cubic yards in five months — about 700 cubic yards per day — using 250 men and 126 oxen.

Twenty-two years later, the Commonwealth of Massachusetts hired the Boston engineering firm of Goss and Munson to fill the Back Bay flats. The contrast with the early operation is stunning. The right-hand photo shows the Needham site where two 25-horsepower steam shovels were at work excavating the local gravel hills. Loaded into dirt cars, the fill was then transported nine miles by rail to Back Bay Boston. In 1858, the *Saturday Evening Gazette* described the scene: "One hundred and forty-five dirt cars, with eighty men, including engineers, brakemen and all, are employed, night and day in loading and transporting the gravel over the road. The trains consist of thirty-five cars each, and make, in the day time, sixteen trips, and in the night nine or ten, or twenty-five in twenty-four hours. Three trains are continually on the road during the day, and one arrives at the Back Bay every forty-five minutes." At this rate, the operation moved about 2500 cubic yards a day, enough to fill two houselots and several times the rate at which Asa Sheldon had taken fill from Pemberton Hill.

This technical bravado was matched by a fiscal *tour-de-force*. When the legislators authorized the state to begin filling its Back Bay lands, they provided no working capital to accomplish the project. Undaunted, the Commonwealth secured start-up funds by selling large plots to private individuals (who profited handsomely from their investments),

View toward Beacon Hill, 1863-1869

then struck a deal with Goss and Munson whereby the contractors took their pay in houselots — working on consignment, as it were, for approximately a quarter of the land they created. When the operation was soundly in the black, the arrangement was altered to pay the contractors directly. Thus the Commonwealth was able to orchestrate a 100-acre real estate development without advancing a penny of its own funds.

As the Back Bay shoreline edged westward, its progress was measured on the first of every month. The contractors were paid accordingly and the new houselots were sold at auction — with strict minimum prices to discourage cheap land use. In the end the state's Back Bay venture would realize a $3.5 million profit, of which half was turned into an education fund.

The operation was strictly regulated: Wooden sewer pipes were laid and then covered with about twenty feet of gravel. Streets were filled to the level of the Mill Dam, seventeen feet above average low tide, but the building lots were left five feet lower, eliminating the need to re-excavate for foundations when houses were built. Construction followed the filling operation by a block or so. The photographs on page 17 give some idea of its progress. By 1860 the shoreline had been extended to Clarendon Street, by 1870 to Exeter, and around 1880 the advance fill was nearing the mainland. The bottom picture is particularly interesting. The prominent house to the right of the State House dome still stands on the corner of Beacon and Dartmouth streets. It dates from 1863, and the next house westward was not constructed until six years later. Among the grove of trees on the right is a group of frame houses; one of these is probably the old Mill Dam tollhouse.

Records of auction prices give some notion of the new land's value. Though prices would fluctuate with economic conditions, the trend was a sure and steady rise. From an 1857 starting point of $1.05 per square foot, the average price for a houselot rose to $1.70 in 1860, $2.80 in 1870, and $3.25 in 1880. The last piece of Commonwealth property was sold in 1886 at $4.35 per square foot. Prices, of course, depended on location; land on Beacon and Commonwealth was more valuable than on Marlborough or Newbury, and there was an additional premium for corner lots.

This discussion has focused almost entirely on the lands belonging to the Commonwealth, which represent about half the modern Back Bay neighborhood. Of the remainder, the Mill Dam property on the north side of Beacon Street was a separate project, proceeding somewhat more rapidly and ruled by fewer restrictions. Thus many water-side properties had stables in the rear, and the houses also display a greater variety in lot size, setbacks, and projections. The rest of Back Bay land, also controlled by Mill Dam interests, was filled under a separate contract with Goss and Munson and was closely coordinated with the work on state lands. As houselots were created, they were sold privately rather than at auction.

THE ARCHITECTS

A vast tract of new houselots, a flush of prosperity and cosmopolitanism, and a generation of erudite young men prepared to break from the past — this was a singular concurrence of circumstances, and it was closely linked to the development of the architectural profession in America.

The connection between the new residential quarter and the new architectural discipline has lent itself to metaphor: The Back Bay was the spawning ground for the local architectural profession, the training field for its recruits, the proving ground for their earliest efforts. Back Bay was the *tabula rasa*, the empty canvas, and the Gilded Age aristocracy that flocked there were the architects' patrons.

Another ingredient in this mix was the presence, after 1864, of the Massachusetts

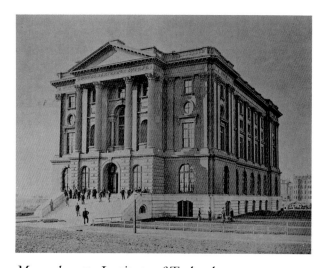

Massachusetts Institute of Technology

Institute of Technology (MIT). One of the earliest institutions in the district, its original building (opposite) was designed by William G. Preston as a companion to his Museum of Natural History (page 17) on land donated by the state. Soon thereafter, MIT president William Barton Rogers invited a young architect named William Robert Ware to organize a school — the first in the nation — offering a formal architectural program.

Accepting the assignment, Ware set off on a fact-finding trip abroad. In London he looked at English institutions, with their emphasis on technology and construction, then moved on to Paris and the famed École des Beaux-Arts. Ware himself had been trained in the Beaux-Arts tradition at the New York atelier-studio of Richard Morris Hunt, the first American graduate of the École. Back at MIT, Ware set up a school modeled roughly on the French system, which opened its doors to students in 1868. (One of them was a poor Boston boy named Louis Sullivan, who left after one year of study, rejecting MIT's formal training as "a mish-mash of architectural theology.")

The next decade was a period of growing erudition within the profession, and with the 1876 debut of *American Architect and Building News,* Boston moved into the forefront of the American architectural scene. This publication, the first American periodical for architects, reflected the prevailing thoughts among Boston architects, and fashions originating in Back Bay became models for urban dwellings across the nation.

Against this background the streets of Back Bay were pushing westward. The early years were dominated by French style and French theory — which itself harked back to the traditions of the Italian Renaissance. The leading exponents of the movement were Arthur Gilman, author of the Back Bay street plan, and his associate Gridley J. Fox Bryant. The French vogue, largely confined to the sixties, is admirably reflected in the mansard blocks on Arlington Street and in Bryant's 20-36 Commonwealth Avenue.

This flirtation with Parisian styles would scarcely survive the decade, and in the seventies the city could be seen turning to its Anglo-Yankee origins and the lure of High Victorian London. Robert S. Peabody, a principal in Boston's most prestigious firm, said

THE CAMERA

These pages present a stunning testimonial to the value of photography in documenting the history of the Back Bay. In the 1880 *Memorial History of Boston,* architect Charles E. Cummings spoke of the camera's role in the district's architectural development:

The introduction of photography just at this time (or rather the rapid perfecting of its processes), and the great extension of foreign travel helped forward the artistic education of architects and the artistic cultivation of great numbers of those upon whom they must depend for encouragement and support. . . . Photography had brought to our hand the examples of Rome and Florence, of Venice and Verona, of Paris and London. Northern Gothic, Southern Gothic, Romanesque, Renaissance — the happy architect could "expatiate free o'er all this scene of man," confident that an appreciative community would salute each new monument as a new triumph.

of his own student days in Paris: "We rendered the French projects, but the thought of England the picturesque was ever present within us." Other Boston architects would define their loyalties as neither French nor English. William Ware's partner Henry Van Brunt voiced the optimism and self-confidence that defined his generation when he declared: "We Americans occupy a new century having no inheritance of ruin and no embarrassment of tradition . . . all the past is ours!" Another prominent architect, Charles E. Cummings, would look back on the Back Bay project as "an

H. H. Richardson, 1884, photo by "Clover" Adams

opportunity . . . for breaking away from the old traditions."

And break away they did. Much of the seventies and most of the eighties were years of extreme individualism as the French-style blocks gave way to rows of highly original and inventive dwellings. The primary inspiration now came from London: in the seventies the writings of John Ruskin and in the eighties the work of architects like Richard Norman Shaw. By 1880, however, the district was also responding to a local influence, the genius of Henry Hobson Richardson (above), whose landmark Trinity Church had been consecrated three years earlier. The final era of Back Bay construction was marked by a new erudition, with an interest in historical prototypes ranging from Classical Greece to Federal New England.

The result of this interplay of styles and sources can be seen on Back Bay streets today: an infinitely fascinating architectural texture, picturesquely detailed yet almost always controlled by a certain degree of discipline. As Bainbridge Bunting noted, within the entire district there are no more than a few Victorian "horrors."

All this architectural history was played out on the streets of Back Bay. The photographs on pages 82 through 91 present an east-to-west tour of the modern district, reflecting a half century of changing tastes in urban domestic architecture. During those years the architectural profession came of age. In 1850, the eve of Back Bay construction, the *Boston City Directory* listed only 32 men who identified themselves as architects; by 1900 the number had swelled to nearly 300. These figures reflect much more than activity in Back Bay, of course. The entire metropolitan area was rapidly expanding, and when the Great Fire of 1872 devastated Boston's downtown business district, there was an instant demand for hundreds of new commercial buildings. Though Boston would eventually lose its pre-eminence as an architectural center, every corner of Back Bay preserves reminders of that golden hour, peopled with the artists and artisans who were in the vanguard of American architecture during its formative years.

INSTITUTIONS

Bostonians of the day were effusive in their praise of the new quarter, which soon was unarguably the city's finest residential district. When the first families of the city established themselves in Back Bay houses, they brought their churches with them. One by one the spires rose above the new mansard roofs, first the Georgian-style Arlington Street Church (page 17), followed by other houses of worship that remain Back Bay landmarks: Emmanuel, the Central Congregational, the First Church, Brattle Square. The typical Back Bay church was picturesque and English — frequently Gothic — and constructed of local puddingstone. Often, if a congregation had abandoned an earlier house of worship, it sentimentally incorporated fragments of the older building into the new.

Two notable variations from this model were churches that stood on opposite corners at Exeter and Newbury streets: the Romanesque First Spiritualist Temple, surviving today as a bookstore, and an odd and graceless structure (opposite) designed for the Hollis Street Church by George F. Meacham, who as a young man had created the prizewinning plan for the Public Garden. The Meacham church has not survived.

On the same corner was the district's first public school, the Prince School (page 27), which opened its doors in 1876. Three years earlier, the Chauncey Hall School for boys had moved from its old downtown location to a fine new schoolhouse on Copley Square (page 23), and for girls there were numerous "home and day schools" operated by proper Back Bay ladies at proper Back Bay addresses.

From the beginning, Back Bay attracted institutions of higher learning. Following the MIT complex on Boylston Street came Harvard Medical School, Boston University, Simmons College, and Massachusetts Normal School (later Massachusetts College of Art). Arriving somewhat later was an institution that would become a major Back Bay presence: Emerson College of Oratory, founded in 1880 to develop public-speaking skills; renamed Emerson College, the school now owns about twenty Back Bay buildings.

An age of prosperity and expansion saw the birth of new cultural facilities: the Museum of Natural History and the Museum of Fine Arts both established themselves on Back Bay land. It was also an age of enthusiasms, and clubs sprung up to serve every inclination: the Boston Art Club, the Algonquin Club, St. Botolph's

Hollis Street Church

Club, the Boston Athletic Club, and a short-lived group devoted to the popular new pastime of cycling. The Massachusetts Bicycle Club's clubhouse, another George F. Meacham design, featured a conveniently ramped entrance arch directly onto Newbury Street (left).

As all these fine institutional buildings rose on prime Back Bay sites, the district emerged as the cultural center of the city which, in the immodest assessment of Beacon Street resident Oliver Wendell Holmes, was already "the thinking center of the continent, and therefore of the planet."

COPLEY SQUARE

The most important cluster of institutional buildings in Back Bay would rise on an unpromising tract abutting the railroad tracks on the southwestern edge of Commonwealth land. As late as 1870 it was still a grim site, remembered as "a desert of dirt, dust, mud and wind."

A small green square had been envisioned for this vicinity since the earliest stages of planning. Its designated name, St. James Park, presaged a bright future, but its locale was shifted from place to place as the more desirable sections of the district were developed. Its size and shape were also altered until it finally took the form of two pieces of leftover land where the diagonal of Huntington Avenue met the Back Bay grid (see map on next page).

In 1869 this dismal place was the scene of a great extravaganza. Known as the National Peace Jubilee, it was organized by a musical

Massachusetts Bicycle Club

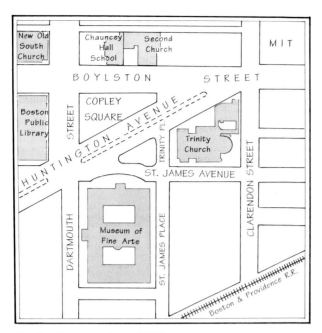

Copley Square, circa 1900

conductor named Patrick S. Gilmore to commemorate the end of the Civil War. For a week in June, Bostonians flocked to the 50,000-seat temporary coliseum pictured below.

The highpoint of this remarkable event was the June 17 performance of the Anvil Chorus from *Il Travatore*, with a chorus of 10,000 and a 1000-piece orchestra. Cannon were fired and church bells rung while 100 firemen beat on anvils with sledgehammers. The four organs were pumped by a relay of twelve men. From this "Niagara of harmony" Boston's leading music critic, John Sullivan Dwight, was said to have "fled to Nahant for the day."

When the flimsy coliseum was battered by

a September storm, it was replaced by a similar structure, where in 1872 Gilmore staged yet another event, this one an International Peace Jubilee to mark the conclusion of the Franco-Prussian War. President Grant made a visit, and the younger Johann Strauss arrived to conduct his own waltzes, but despite these celebrity appearances this jubilee lost money.

But Copley Square would see better days. In 1870 the site of the first coliseum was granted to the new Museum of Fine Arts. Designed by London-trained John H. Sturgis and completed in 1876, the new museum (opposite) was a polychromatic Ruskin Gothic structure liberally ornamented with imported terracotta. In the assessment of one critic, it was "an English building with Italian detail and enough mistakes to make it entirely American"; Boston tastemaker Thomas Gold Appleton called it "frozen Yankee Doodle."

During the next two decades today's Copley Square, in the words of historian Walter Muir Whitehill, "stumbled into shape." The Second Church and Chauncey Hall School (opposite) both appeared in 1873. Facing the museum building, its Ruskinian soulmate, the "new" Old South Church, rose across the square. Completed in 1875, it was the design of Charles A. Cummings, who here created one of the most picturesque profiles of the era (right). It was crowned by a towering campanile, which soon after completion began to lean to the southwest. In 1931, when the tower was about three feet out of line and threatening to collapse, it was demolished and rebuilt with a somewhat lower and less flamboyant silhouette.

Peace Jubilee Coliseum, 1869

New Old South Church

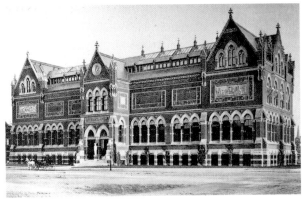

Museum of Fine Arts

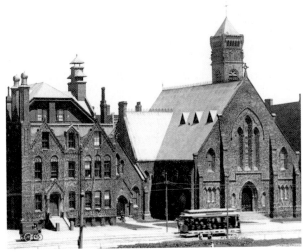

Chauncey Hall School and Second Church

With the arrival of the MFA, the open parcel in front of the museum became known as Art Square. In 1883 the name was officially designated Copley Square in honor of Boston's eighteenth-century expatriate artist. About the same time a second, smaller piece of land was added to the original "square" — which now became two triangles intersected by Huntington Avenue.

THE GREAT ONES

We now turn to the buildings for which Copley Square is famous: H. H. Richardson's Trinity Church and Charles F. McKim's Boston Public Library. These two structures are distinguished from their neighbors not only by their monumentality, but by their very essence. Both were conceived and executed as total works of art, and to be fully appreciated they must be seen inside as well as out. Fortunately, both buildings are ordinarily open to the public every day of the week.

By Richardson's own account, he drew the plan for Trinity from various historical sources. The great square tower was inspired by the Old Cathedral in Salamanca, Spain, and the massing and decorative motifs from the Romanesque

architecture of the Auvergne region of central France. The Greek Cross of the floor plan is derived from churches from Byzantium to Renaissance Italy. Deftly combining these various elements, Richardson created the striking new approach to Romanesque design that would become synonymous with his name.

Trinity parish, founded in 1733 as the third Anglican church in Boston, purchased this plot in 1872. A competition the same year awarded the commission to Richardson, who subsequently moved his architectural practice from New York to Boston. Though five years would pass before the church was consecrated, the parish made an unexpected early move to Back Bay when their building in downtown Boston was destroyed in the Great Fire of November 1872. Until the parish house was completed two years later, services were held nearby in an MIT lecture hall.

Richardson called Trinity his "color church," and he entrusted its interior decoration to his friend John La Farge, the inventor of the opalescent glass commonly associated with Tiffany Studios. For this project La Farge assembled a talented team of artists and craftsmen, including a young Augustus Saint-Gaudens, who was employed painting and stenciling the new plaster walls. Five windows were designed by La Farge and four by Sir Edward Burne-Jones. Together with mosaics, murals, fine woods, and carved stone, they create a richly textured interior that admirers have compared to St. Mark's in Venice.

Another young man involved in the Trinity project was Charles Follen McKim, a draftsman in the Richardson office. A decade later McKim returned to Copley Square to design his own building, in which the collaborative decorative approach pioneered at Trinity produced interiors that would be praised as "the veritable Assisi of American art."

The serene splendor of the Boston Public Library belies the controversy that surrounded almost every step of its design. The library acquired the Copley Square site in 1880. There followed several years of wrangling between the city, which favored a neo-Romanesque design by Boston's municipal architect, and the library trustees, who envisioned something quite different. In 1887 the commission was finally awarded to the trustees' choice, the distinguished New York firm of McKim, Mead and White. The partner in charge of the project was Charles McKim, who shared entirely the trustees' commitment to creating an extraordinary building — a "palace for the people" aglitter with "art for the sake of ART."

To this end McKim recruited an all-star cast including the brothers Augustus and Louis Saint-Gaudens, Daniel Chester French, Pierre Puvis de Chavannes, Edwin Austin Abbey, and John Singer Sargent.

As work progressed, McKim and the trustees continued to press a reluctant, frequently hostile city, urging always that more time and more money be committed to their elaborate decorative program. Indeed, the fervor that motivated these men has been likened to the spirit that inspired medieval communities to build their great cathedrals. In the end the original budget of $450,000 would exceed $2.5 million — though a large part of this sum came from private contributions, much of it raised personally by McKim. Moreover, the final figures show a slim fee of $22,000 to McKim, Mead and White for eight years of services.

The final controversy seems a typically Bostonian episode. The four wings of McKim's library surrounded a cloistered courtyard. In 1894 the architect announced his desire to install in the court a sculpture by Frederick MacMonnies as a gift in memory of his wife, Julia Appleton. Known as *Bacchante and Infant Faun*, the piece (opposite) ultimately caused an uproar, fiercely attacked as an offense to temperance, motherhood, and female decency. McKim subsequently revoked his gift and gave the statue to New York's Metropolitan Museum. Today, a copy of the *Bacchante* occupies a niche in a corridor of the library building, awaiting transfer to the courtyard when the current restoration is complete.

McKim's library plan also addressed the

Trinity Church, west towers removed

Boston Public Library

eliminated Huntington Avenue to achieve an actual square. Following a subsequent redesign in the 1980s, Copley Square has perhaps finally achieved its form and identity as a truly effective urban space in the heart of the Back Bay neighborhood.

THE RESIDENTS

"One of the grandest architectural sections in the world," gushes the 1880 *King's Guide to Boston*. Its avenues are "the most fashionable thoroughfares of the aristocratic Bostonians." Whenever Victorian Boston speaks of Back Bay, one encounters this extravagant kind of

The Bacchante, 1896

triangle of land fronting the library, for which he envisioned an open plaza with a large central fountain. This design was never executed. For about a hundred years the space received various treatments, from the patch of grass upon which bicyclists posed (below) to the well-tended parterre that appeared somewhat later. The square remained two separate triangles until 1969, when a major redesign

Copley Square, 1902

Bicyclists and Trinity Church, with original west towers (before 1886 fire)

The Burrage Mansion

language — the image of a sumptuous residential quarter inhabited by the city's first and finest families.

In fact, not all of aristocratic Boston moved to the new land. Some remained on Beacon Hill while others were drawn to the suburbs. But many of the older families did arrive, and here they encountered some new neighbors — prosperous merchants and self-made moguls newly rich from ventures in a burgeoning industrial economy.

There was a well-known formula that sought to define the social geography of the early Back Bay: Beacon Street, it said, was the home of persons with both family and money. Marlborough Street was for those with family connections but limited wealth. Commonwealth Avenue was for people with perhaps more money than pedigree, and Newbury Street for those who possessed neither.

The two photographs on this page happen to fit this formula neatly. At right are adjoining houses that once stood on Beacon Street, the homes of business partners C. A. Whittier and Francis Lee Higginson. Both buildings date from 1881, the Whittier house designed by McKim, Mead and White and Higginson's by H. H. Richardson — proper residences for proper Bostonians. The photo above shows the mock château that was erected at 314 Commonwealth Avenue for a Harvard-educated Californian named Albert C. Burrage,

who after a successful career as a gas company executive made a second fortune in copper. Completed in 1899, the Burrage mansion seems to have elicited muted snickers from parlors on Beacon Street.

Only a few such lavish houses were ever built. All across Back Bay one encounters rows of relatively modest homes, typically erected by developers either for resale or as rental properties. This kind of speculation accounts for more than half of Back Bay building, but of the speculators themselves, little is known beyond their names. Bainbridge Bunting's research identifies some of the major builders, men like Fred Pope, an architect-developer who erected more than fifty buildings over a twenty-year period, and Silas Merrill, who built that many properties on Newbury Street alone. Charles Freeland, already prosperous from South End ventures, arrived early in Back Bay to erect his own Beacon Street residence, then stayed on to build several dozen more. The most prolific builder of the era was George Wheatland from Salem, whose name is associated with almost one hundred Back Bay properties.

More than a showcase of Boston's rich and famous, nineteenth-century Back Bay was a place where people lived and through which they moved in the routines of their daily lives. The photographs on the opposite page offer a few glimpses of that place, with its appealing blend of decorum and domesticity in its glory days.

Houses of F. L. Higginson (left) and C. A. Whittier (right)

23 Commonwealth Avenue

Winter scene on Arlington Street

"The Little Green Car" on Marlborough Street

Morning Exercise at the Prince School, 1893

Commonwealth Avenue near Clarendon Street

212 Commonwealth Avenue

Significantly, the decades of Back Bay's development coincided with spectacular improvements in both building technology and the comforts of everyday life. In fact, these circumstances probably spurred the success of the Back Bay venture, as houses built just a generation earlier became suddenly obsolete. The excellent documentation of the 1860 Gibson House Museum reveals that this building — among the very first Back Bay residences — was equipped with full plumbing facilities, a coal-fueled central heating system, and gas lighting fixtures throughout the house. For a well-to-do family, erecting such a home in the popular new district was an attractive alternative to updating an older place.

Behind more-or-less uniform facades, the style-conscious owner could create his personal decor, choosing mass-manufactured woodwork and fittings from profusely illustrated catalogs. Thus the interior of the Gibson House is quite distinct from that of its twin next door, which was more elaborately and expensively fitted. The organization of rooms in the two houses also differed, reflecting the different needs of the two families.

In both buildings, however, the room arrangement reflects a similar sense of social order. The public areas of the first and second floors are considerably more formal and decorative than the family rooms upstairs, and the servants' areas below stairs and in the attic, though comfortable, are plain and functional.

As with the streetscape, Back Bay flirted briefly with the Parisian mode of horizontal

Hotel Vendome, 1875

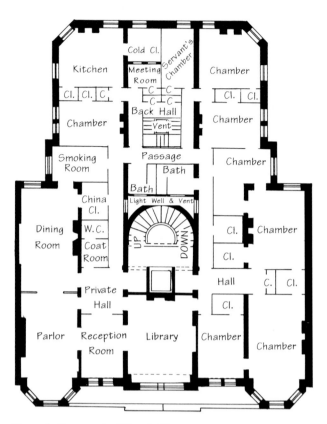

French flat at the Hotel Cluny

living. "French flats" combined luxury accommodations with the most modern conveniences of the day. Among the best known was the Hotel Agassiz, a grand affair financed by the noted philanthropist Henry Lee Higginson to house himself and five other families in spacious floor-through flats. Seen above is a floor plan for a fifteen-room apartment in another prestigious French flat building, the Hotel Cluny. Other establishments, like the Vendome (below) offered both transient and residential suites with hotel-style dining facilities.

Though these alternatives enjoyed a certain popularity — there were once about twenty of them in Back Bay alone — they were jocularly identified as the habitat of the "newly wed and nearly dead." Between these two conditions, most Back Bay residents apparently retained a lingering prejudice against cohabiting with other families under the same roof.

In the beginning it appears that decisions about interior decor were shared by the homeowner and the architect. As years passed, however, wealthier patrons began to seek the services of professional designers, like New Yorkers Christian Herter and Louis Comfort

Drawing room in the Oliver Ames house, 355 Commonwealth Avenue

Dinner at the J. L. Gardners', 152 Beacon Street

Oliver Wendell Holmes, Sr., at 296 Beacon Street

Charles Hammond Gibson and John P. Marquand in 137 Beacon Street

Commonwealth Avenue Mall, circa 1880

is the number and size of the trees. Indeed, the twentieth-century greening of Back Bay was so complete that the district's major chronicler, Bainbridge Bunting, complained that it was "choked with trees," obstructing architectural photography or even architectural viewing.

Old photos show that except for the Commonwealth Avenue Mall (at left), trees were not a feature of early Back Bay streets, nor for that matter were the small front yards treated as gardens. The early view of Marlborough Street (below), the leafiest of modern streets, clearly makes this point. By the 1870s summering had become fashionable, and most Back Bay houses were used only as winter residences — from nineteenth-century reminiscences, one senses that the seasonal Bostonian often considered his country house the family's true home; the town house was merely a snug accommodation during the foul weather of the social season.

By 1900, a few scattered street trees had made an appearance, and soon thereafter some systematic plantings were undertaken to beautify the urban landscape. And although tree-lined streets and well-tended gardens were not the vision of Back Bay's planners, few would advocate a radical pruning. Most urban dwellers appreciate the greenery.

The four small parks once projected for the Back Bay neighborhood never materialized. Instead, the district received a broad ribbon of parkland along its northern perimeter. The development of this riverside area, today's Charles River Esplanade, occurred over several decades, and in a sense it represents the final phase of the Back Bay saga.

Tiffany or the Bostonian Ogden Codman, who designed and decorated mansions from Newport to the French Riviera. With the 1880s came extravagantly elegant interiors, usually drawn from the styles of aristocratic Europe. Then as always, the public was fascinated with the rich and famous, whose homes were showcased in books and magazines. The Oliver Ames mansion, for example, was included in an 1883 compendium of *Artistic Houses.* The house (page 29) exemplified Gilded Age splendor. Just as often, however, the old pictures reveal comfortable, cluttered rooms of considerable individuality and charm.

"CHOKED WITH TREES"
Perhaps the most striking difference between the early Back Bay streets and those of today

Marlborough Street, circa 1870

"New Boston and Charles River Bay," proposal by Charles Davenport

THE ESPLANADE

Filling in the bay did not solve the problem of sewage on the mud flats; it only transferred the unpleasantness onto the marshy fringes of the Charles. Moreover, the river itself remained a saltwater estuary, fluctuating with the tides and prone to flooding. The center picture at right shows the view from the rear of 204 Beacon Street during a storm in November 1898. A note accompanying the picture says that it was taken "before the highest of the tide." The reminiscence continues: "When there was a run of high tides and the wind was right, the water came under the house, and forced up a trap door in the front basement room. . . . Later it would find its level in the shed and kitchen at the back. It never put out the furnace as it did in other houses. . . ."

The solution to all these woes was developed over several decades, beginning in 1893, when the river bank was extended with a 100-foot promenade, seen at right as it was in 1911. The year before this photo was taken, the river's water level had been stabilized by a tidal dam. Finally, the Storrow Embankment created a broad strip of parkland, based roughly upon the Alster Basin in the German city of Hamburg — and strikingly similar to an 1874 proposal (above) by Charles Davenport, who then owned vast tracts on the Cambridge side of the river. This project was finally accomplished in 1931. Twenty years later a highway would cut

Flooding behind Beacon Street, 1898

The Esplanade, 1911

between Back Bay and the river, but it was Boston's good fortune that the parkland was partially preserved.

In the early 1880s, Frederick Law Olmsted had carried out his vast improvements of the Muddy River and the Fens. Thus, in the twentieth century the Back Bay neighborhood was bounded to the east, west, and north by parkland — the Public Garden, the Fens, the Esplanade. And although the southern perimeter consisted of ugly railroad yards, even these provided an effective boundary. In the view of Bainbridge Bunting, it was these four clearly defined borders that preserved and protected the Back Bay district: "This enabled the district to retain for a long time its character as a high-grade residential quarter and finally to make an orderly transition to an area of offices and apartments." Moreover, "Because of Arthur Gilman's Commonwealth Avenue, because of Frederick Law Olmsted's park system, and because of the open stretches of the Charles River, the twentieth-century inhabitant, standing in the heart of the city and looking out onto sprawling modern Boston, can enjoy the restorative qualities of space and greenery so rare in other urban districts."

Within these protective boundaries, Back Bay survived its twentieth-century transition from a place of fashion to a student quarter. In retrospect, it seems that another key to this survival was benign neglect, as buildings became rundown but were seldom replaced. A progressive shabbiness overspread much of the district, which according to one reminiscence soon resembled "one big college campus."

The turnaround probably dates from the 1950s, when forces were joined to oppose high-rise apartment houses. It was a hard-won battle, but it led to height limits for all residential areas. In 1955 the Neighborhood Association of the Back Bay was formed to promote the interests of residents, its primary aim that "Back Bay will be recognized once more as the most desirable district in Boston."

In 1966 this goal was boosted by the creation of the Back Bay Architectural District, with the Back Bay Architectural Commission to oversee all exterior changes to neighborhood structures. Thus, except for disastrous events such as the fire that ravaged Ware and Van Brunt's First Church (below), further destruction of nineteenth-century buildings should be prevented.

Today an extensive network of community activists works in public-private partnership with city government to protect and enhance the architectural treasure that sprang from the mud flats of the original "back" bay.

— GAIL WEESNER

The First Church, erected 1867

March 22, 1968

Back Bay Today

Neighborhood residents at work and at play

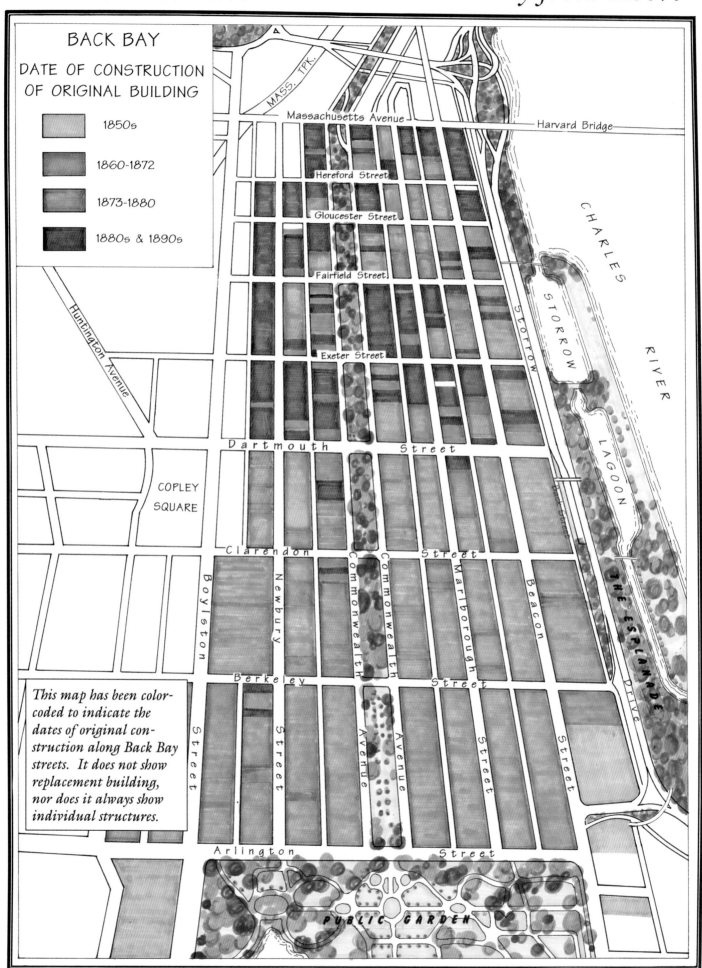

BACK BAY

DATE OF CONSTRUCTION
OF ORIGINAL BUILDING

1850s

1860-1872

1873-1880

1880s & 1890s

MASS. TPK.

Massachusetts Avenue — Harvard Bridge —

Hereford Street

Gloucester Street

Fairfield Street

Exeter Street

Huntington Avenue

D a r t m o u t h   S t r e e t

COPLEY
SQUARE

CHARLES

STORROW

RIVER

LAGOON

Back Street

C l a r e n d o n   S t r e e t

THE ESPLANADE

Boylston   Street

Newbury   Street

Commonwealth

Commonwealth   Avenue

Avenue

Marlborough   Street

Beacon   Street

Berkeley   Street

This map has been color-
coded to indicate the
dates of original con-
struction along Back Bay
streets. It does not show
replacement building,
nor does it always show
individual structures.

Arlington   Street

P U B L I C   G A R D E N

BEACON STREET
Mill Dam

BEACON STREET RUNS along the 1821 toll road and mill dam that once spanned the Back Bay flats, separating them from the tidal waters of the Charles River and providing Boston with a new link to the mainland at Brookline. Thus, the street originated as a thoroughfare, a role it continues to play.

Officially called Western Avenue, the old road was commonly known as Mill Dam. On the eve of Back Bay development, it was renamed Beacon Street, thereby acquiring the aristocratic associations of the older Beacon Hill end of the street, and it soon became the symbol of proper Victorian Boston.

While the other Back Bay streets inched westward with the progress of the fill, Beacon Street marched rapidly across the existing causeway, and by 1870 new houses had risen as far west as Hereford Street. Consequently, this street does not exhibit the orderly progression of architectural styles seen elsewhere in Back Bay. Rather, it is dominated by the crisp brownstone facades associated with the 1860s.

To Beacon Street resident Oliver Wendell Holmes, it was "the sunny street that holds the sifted few," and the south-facing waterside has always been more desirable; around 1960 two high-rise apartment buildings were erected to take advantage of the sun and the water view. Height restrictions soon followed.

The street is also the haunt of students from Back Bay's numerous schools and colleges. Emerson and Fisher colleges alone own more than twenty Beacon Street buildings.

NOTED RESIDENTS:
Isabella Stewart Gardner, collector Numbers 150-152
Oliver Wendell Holmes, Sr., physician, author Numbers 294-296
Julia Ward Howe, author Number 241
William Dean Howells, author Number 302
William Morris Hunt, artist Number 405
George Santayana, philosopher, poet Number 302

House of Apley. Six dwellings in a row at 198-208 Beacon Street are typical of the French academic buildings that rose atop the Mill Dam in the 1860s. Like most early Back Bay houses, they were built on speculation, their architect unknown. One of the houses in this row is reputed to have been the fictional residence of "The Late George Apley."

Unidentical twins. The dwellings at 135 and 137 Beacon Street were probably the first houses erected on the Commonwealth's Back Bay land, begun in 1859 for merchant Samuel H. Russell and his aunt, a 56-year-old widow named Catherine Hammond Gibson. Though the facades are almost identical, the interiors are quite different. The architect was Edward Clark Cabot, whose firm Cabot and Chandler would subsequently design some twenty Back Bay houses. In 1957, Number 137 was established as a Victorian museum through the bequest of Charles Hammond Gibson, poet, eccentric, and grandson of the original owner.

A famous address. For forty years the site of 150-152 Beacon Street was the home of "Boston's most cherished institution" and "queen of holy Back Bay," Isabella Stewart Gardner. "Mrs. Jack" lived here during her collecting years, amassing much of the art she later moved to her new home on the Fenway. The white stone mansion that replaced Mrs. Gardner's two houses was built in 1904 for industrialist Eben S. Draper, who served two years as governor of Massachusetts, and in the 1920s it was the home of another governor, Alvan T. Fuller. Today it is the Emerson College library.

Survivor. Despite some major tampering at the entry level and again at the roofline, 166 Beacon Street is still an eye-catcher. Its geometric stonework and the herringbone pattern defining the original cornice line were the 1882 design of Cabot and Chandler. A comparison between this richly patterned facade and that of E. C. Cabot's 135-137 Beacon Street (opposite) tells much about the course of Back Bay architecture since 1860.

Gothic brownstone. Somber in crumbling brownstone, the house at 165 Beacon Street is one of a handful of Back Bay houses with a Gothic flavor — pointed arches, carved tracery, and a steeply pitched roof with a fanciful wooden gable. The lower part of the bay has recently been painted, presumably to protect the stone. The dominant building material of the 1860s, brownstone is soft and easy to carve but has poor resistance to Boston weather, being prone to cracking and flaking.

Showplace. The stunning facade at 170 Beacon Street was the 1900 design of Ogden Codman, the architect/decorator who with fellow-tastemaker Edith Wharton wrote the Gilded Age guide to style, The Decoration of Houses. Here in Back Bay, Codman created an Adamesque facade and fastidiously planned interiors for financier and collector Eben Howard Gay as a showplace for his prized collection of Chippendale furniture. Both Gay and Codman traveled to Europe to gather ideas and materials for the house, buying up doors, mantelpieces, and hardware. In 1966 the building was acquired by the Federal Republic of Germany; it is the headquarters of Goethe-Institut, a German cultural center.

Avant-garde. Although the Boston Public Library is commonly cited as the first Renaissance-style building in Boston, this mansion at 266 Beacon Street was begun in 1886, a full year before Charles F. McKim was commissioned to design the BPL. It was the work of the Boston firm of Shaw and Hunnewell, and its 40-foot limestone facade gave the architects a broad canvas upon which to display their competent handling of Renaissance detail: fluted pilasters, swags, lions' heads, and a fourth floor recessed behind a balustrade topped with classical urns.

High-rise. The 17-story apartment building at 330 Beacon Street was completed in 1959 and recalls the battles that raged throughout the sixties, as residents and preservationists rallied to the threat of runaway high-rise development. In the end, a 65-foot height restriction was adopted for most of Back Bay. Containing 80 condominium units, this is one of the largest residential buildings in the district. Waterside apartments offer spectacular views of the Charles River, Cambridge, and the western hills.

347 Beacon. The name of architect J. H. Besarick is identified with more than a dozen Back Bay houses, most of them slightly eccentric. Here at the corner of Fairfield Street, he designed a brick-and-brownstone dwelling that Bainbridge Bunting called "the most elaborate if not the most successful Romanesque house in the district." The stonework of the arched entry, the frieze above the first-floor windows, and the balustrade of the entry steps (above) are garnished with carved botanical motifs, which in some sections are badly weathered.

334 Beacon. Behind this picturesque facade is an 1871 red brick house built by architect/developer Fred Pope. Pope was among the major builders in the district and was particularly active along this part of Beacon Street, where he sometimes took up residence. At one time he could have stood on this site and seen some thirty buildings of his own design. In 1907, this house was remodeled as a mini-château by the firm of Cram and Goodhue. Ralph Adams Cram was a self-taught architect who was an art critic and medieval scholar as well as one of the most influential designers of his day.

Aristocrats. The row of houses numbered 403-409 Beacon has suffered sorely from neglect, and more particularly from the loss of Number 401, the fifth house in an architectural ensemble from 1867. The architects, George Snell and J. R. Gregerson, created some of the handsomest houses in the district, typically in the style that Bunting called "Brick Academic." Even these shabby survivors retain a graceful dignity that identifies them as aristocrats. The three central buildings are tied together with continuous iron balconies with a delicate fleur-de-lis motif. Number 403 was the residence of the architect Gregerson, and painter William Morris Hunt once lived at Number 405.

New England School of Optometry. The four separate buildings owned by the New England School of Optometry were erected between 1892 and 1904. All are faced with limestone, and they represent the work of three prominent architectural firms and three stylistic currents present in Back Bay near the turn of the century. In the foreground is Number 420, in pure Italian Renaissance style, the 1892 work of Peabody and Stearns; Number 422, 1899, is an Adamesque design by Little and Browne; and Numbers 424 and 426 are a 1904 Baroque pair by Julius Schweinfurth. NESO is one of several Back Bay schools that have taken pride in preserving their historic buildings.

Trading places. These two buildings have curiously opposed histories. On the left is 448 Beacon, in yellow brick and reddish sandstone and dating from 1889. Its shell cornice was inspired by the château of Chambord, and its curriculum vitae is long and varied. A residence until the twenties, it subsequently served as Masonic lodge, restaurant, school, and since 1974 as headquarters for the Church of Scientology. At the western end of the same block is Church Court, an 1891 house of worship converted to residences. After a 1978 fire, it was rebuilt as 42 condominiums, with a seven-story vertical unit in the tower.

Hotel Cambridge. Improvements in the passenger elevator in the late 1880s spurred an era of high-rise construction, particularly of multi-unit "family hotels." Some of the most imposing of these structures were erected at the western edges of the Back Bay district. Here at 483 Beacon is architect Willard T. Sears's Hotel Cambridge, rising ten floors to a stylish mansard emblazoned with the monogram "HC." While completing this building, Sears also embarked on his long, sometimes painful association with Isabella Stewart Gardner, designing and redesigning Fenway Court.

MARLBOROUGH STREET
Lovely and Livable

NESTLED BETWEEN austere Beacon Street and proud Commonwealth Avenue, Marlborough Street offers a comfortable blend of loveliness and livability. Moreover, it retains a greater degree of its original character than any other street in the district. Along its entire length, there are only a few buildings that are not original structures. Narrower with smaller houselots, it has an ambiance of friendly domesticity, and because it is not a thoroughfare (ending at the Public Garden on the east and Charlesgate on the west), it is the quietest Back Bay street.

West of Dartmouth the scale becomes even more intimate with green and shady front yards and smaller, unpretentious houses that are well suited to modern family living. Many of Back Bay's fifty single-family residences are on upper Marlborough.

In addition to the assorted notables listed below, several architects seem to have lived on the street: Gridley J. F. Bryant (Number 66), Russell Sturgis (190), Francis W. Chandler (195), Henry Van Brunt (292), and Willard T. Sears (322). So did MIT's founding president William Barton Rogers (117) and Harvard president Abbott Lawrence Lowell (171).

Marlborough Street was the route of the "Little Green Car," the last horse-drawn trolley to operate in the city, which made its final run on Christmas Eve 1900. It appears frequently in old photos, like the one on page 27.

NOTED RESIDENTS:

Henry Adams, historian Number 91
Robert Lowell, poet Number 239
Perle Mesta, hostess Number 241
Edwin O'Connor, author Number 10
Katherine Lane Weems, sculptress Number 53

Pleasant scenery. A comely, agreeable character pervades upper Marlborough Street. Tree-lined sidewalks and tidy front yards combine with trim Victorian town houses to form some of Boston's most pleasant urban scenery.

Violation? The gracious entry at 17 Marlborough is admired for its dignified, symmetrical placement of a bay window on a narrow facade. It probably also violates a deed restriction that no projection extend more than five feet beyond the main building line. Bainbridge Bunting suggests that because this houselot was sold in 1862, a year before stringent restrictions were enacted, the violation was not challenged. However, the design was never used again.

A French connection. The five brick-and-sandstone houses at 22-30 Marlborough are handsome examples of Bunting's Brick Academic style, which appeared very early on Back Bay streets. Bunting also points out that this group, dating from 1863, closely resembles the Hospice des Incurables in suburban Paris, designed by the distinguished French architect Théodore Labrouste at about the same time. The regularly spaced arches of alternating doors and windows give the impression of an arcade, a much-admired theme from contemporary Europe.

The French Library. Of four imposing structures that once overlooked the intersection of Marlborough and Berkeley streets, 53 Marlborough is the only one that survives intact. Dating from 1867, it was designed by Sturgis and Brigham, an architectural firm whose commissions spanned three decades and included some of the district's costliest dwellings. For almost fifty years this was the home of sculptress Katherine Lane Weems, who gave the building to the French Library in 1961. The first-floor salon is said to have been inspired by one of the Empress Josephine's private rooms at Malmaison.

Panel brickwork. Glimpsed through the treetops is a vibrant display of panel brickwork at 63 Marlborough Street. The house was the work of J. Pickering Putnam, a European-trained architect who was responsible for some of Back Bay's most exuberant designs. A popular idiom of the seventies, panel brickwork could be restrained (page 84), or exceedingly lively as in this example from 1877.

110-130 Marlborough. This row of 1868 houses is more interesting than it appears, but its architectural theme is so understated that one can miss it completely. Eleven narrow houses form five separate units, with slightly projecting pavilions at the center (seen here) and at both ends. There are other subtle differences in fenestration and at the roofline, but the entire ensemble is staid and subtle, its dominant feature the orderly procession of oriel windows at the second-floor level. The architect of these houses is unknown.

Bowfronts. The bowfront, or swellfront, originated in Georgian England, and arrived in Boston about 1810. Though some Victorian architects regretted "its wearisome pertinacity," it never fell totally from favor. This 1869 house at 93 Marlborough Street sported two great bows flanking a center entry that survives as a window. The house once belonged to Henry Adams. Today known as Hale House, it is combined with several adjoining buildings as a retirement home for about fifty residents. It is named for nineteenth-century Boston's beloved preacher, Edward Everett Hale.

The Cushing-Endicott House. Still known by the names of the only two families to occupy this mansion, 163 Marlborough Street is among the most-admired houses in the district. Designed by Snell and Gregerson in 1871, it was built for Thomas C. Cushing, a China Trade merchant who embellished his new home with imported Oriental woodwork and fittings that remain in place today. Facing Marlborough Street is a broad colonnaded porch crowned with a lovely iron balustrade (at left). The mansion wraps gracefully around the corner onto Dartmouth Street, where it forms an ensemble with two other houses.

Tour de force. Sadly disfigured by a twentieth-century roof-raising, the house at 135 Marlborough Street still gives a hint of its original charm. It dates from 1880, when Boston's interest in French fashion had given way to the spirit of the English Queen Anne movement. In that spirit, Cabot and Chandler created a house that would have fit nicely onto many London streets of the day. The cut-brick sunburst panel above the second-floor window was a favored Queen Anne design, which along with another cheerful motif, the sunflower, appears often along Back Bay streets.

Noteworthy.   Listed on the National Register of Historic Places, 164 Marlborough is noteworthy because it is a very early work of Henry Hobson Richardson, a commission from his Harvard friend Benjamin Crowninshield.   Critics tend to be kind about this effort, noting that it reveals the young man's interest in combining various materials — tiles, ironwork, panel brickwork — for decorative effect.   The wrought-iron hood over the entryway is not original to the house; it is absent from the 1870s photo on page 30. The building now serves as a dormitory.

Stylish.   The stylish facade at 191 Marlborough dates from 1881, the design of Carl Fehmer, an architect whose Back Bay career spans two decades and numbers some two dozen buildings.   This is one of the most distinguished.   Only three stories high, it nestles comfortably on an extra-wide lot, giving it a more solid, horizontal feeling than most of its neighbors.   Combining features of the Ruskin Gothic and Queen Anne styles, it has always been admired for its graceful design and high quality of craftsmanship — the carved stone around the door, the balustrades at the entryway, and the wrought-iron grille over the arched porch.

284-292 Marlborough. These five houses from 1872 form another ensemble that has suffered from the vicissitudes of time — in this case by a wayward roof deck and a coat of grey paint over one of the towered end houses. The architects, Ware and Van Brunt, had impeccable Back Bay credentials. William Ware founded the MIT School of Architecture, and Henry Van Brunt was noted for his architectural writings. The three center houses mark the first appearance of the Dutch gable in Back Bay.

334 Marlborough. Here is another product of the ingenious J. H. Besarick, who assumes a lighter touch in this cheerful-looking brick residence dating from 1872. Though it gives the impression of a freestanding house, its rear wall is attached to a row of three small houses fronting Gloucester Street. Only three stories high, this dwelling seems not entirely urban, its roof treatment reminiscent of stick-style cottages then rising in nearby suburbs.

COMMONWEALTH AVENUE
Grande Dame

OUTLINING HIS BACK BAY proposal in 1858, Arthur Gilman described a "noble central avenue" with a spacious tree-lined mall — the kind of monumental thoroughfare popular in European capitals of the day. This street would be the site of the finest new mansions, setting a tone of elegance for the entire district.

Gilman's grand boulevard was laid out with a spaciousness that must have dazzled Bostonians. A 100-foot-wide mall was flanked by carriage roads, beyond which the grand new residences were set back an additional 20 feet — providing a dramatic sweep of 240 feet between housefronts. It was a world removed from the cramped and crooked byways of the old peninsula.

Commonwealth Avenue would fulfill Gilman's cosmopolitan vision. Louis Mumford declared it "the most successful example of nineteenth-century urbanity in the whole country," and it served as a model for boulevards across America. Linking the parklands of the Public Garden with those of the Fens, it would form a precious link in Frederick Law Olmsted's "Emerald Necklace," Boston's metropolitan park system.

The boulevard soon became popular for joy rides and as a route to the open country, and before 1890 there were grumblings about traffic and speeding. And though these complaints would only intensify, Commonwealth Avenue has somehow managed to preserve a sense of decorum. Its grand old mansions have been converted to other uses, but the avenue remains primarily a residential street — the geographic and symbolic heart of Back Bay and its proudest thoroughfare.

NOTED RESIDENTS:

Charles Francis Adams, economist, historian Gloucester Street corner

Oliver Ames, industrialist, governor Number 355

Fanny Farmer, author, cook Hereford Street corner

Henry Lee Higginson, financier, philanthropist Number 191

Commonwealth Avenue Mall. One hundred feet wide and almost a mile long, the Commonwealth Avenue Mall carries a broad swath of parkland through the heart of the Back Bay neighborhood.

A tale of two houses. Numbers 3 and 5 Commonwealth Avenue were once mirror images of each other. Erected in 1861, they were among the finest new residences in the district. About fifty years later their paths diverged when Number 5 (left) was rebuilt in the Beaux-Arts style. The new owner, industrialist Walter C. Baylies, soon added a ballroom on an open plot west of his house. This still-resplendent mansion, its ballroom intact (page 105), now houses the Boston Center for Adult Education. The neighboring dwelling, meanwhile, has retained its original appearance. Today it serves as the French consulate.

20-36 Commonwealth Avenue. Beneath a continuous mansard, these nine houses present a unified facade 175 feet long, broken only by nine oriel windows. Dating from 1861, they are the collaboration of two men who played a key role in Boston architecture, Arthur Gilman and Gridley J. Fox Bryant. The following year the two men designed Boston's new (now old) City Hall on School Street. Whereas Gilman soon moved to New York, Bryant remained in Boston as head of the city's largest architectural firm. It is said that when the 1872 fire destroyed 152 of Bryant's commercial buildings, the firm rebuilt 111!

Magnolias. The first large-scale planting of magnolia trees on Commonwealth Avenue dates from 1963. Today their late-April blooms are Boston's surest sign of spring.

Haddon Hall. To guarantee the dignity of the new district, all Back Bay houses were required to be at least three stories high. But this 1894 residential hotel at 29 Commonwealth Avenue presented a new problem, and revised legislation soon followed. The eleven-story high-rise was designed by J. Pickering Putnam, who built the first three levels in the same style as neighboring brownstones; above, it is a brick tower with banks of bay windows facing the avenue. Once dubbed "the dentists' building," it is now fully occupied by business and professional suites.

A handsome pair. Like the brick row on the opposite page, 25 and 27 Commonwealth Avenue are thought to be designed by Gilman and Bryant. This handsome pair was erected in 1861 for merchant and congressman Samuel Hooper, and despite subsequent alterations this corner, enclosed by the original stone fence, has not changed much. For fifty years both buildings have been owned by Massachusetts General Hospital. Number 25 is maintained as a residence for hospital executives while its larger neighbor, known as Halcyon Place, is a residence for families of hospital patients.

Clarendon Street Playground. This is the site of the Hotel Hamilton, Back Bay's first luxury French flat building. When it was demolished in 1959, neighbors stepped in to block a threatened high-rise overlooking Commonwealth Avenue. In the course of a twenty-year impasse, the empty lot became a temporary playground, which in 1979 received official status. This happy solution is the joint venture of the city and the Neighborhood Association of the Back Bay, with the latter responsible for funding and maintenance.

Back Bay Baroque. Even today, the Beaux-Arts-style houses at 128 and 130 Commonwealth Avenue seem a bit out of place in the heart of Back Bay Boston. In fact, their elaborate stone fronts have overlooked the avenue since 1905, when two red brick dwellings were remodeled with a Fifth Avenue flair. After several decades of institutional use, the pair has recently been converted back to housing — an encouraging sign of the renewed vitality of the residential neighborhood.

The Vendome. The venerable Vendome was erected in two stages. The original building, designed by William G. Preston in 1871, was a small residential hotel facing Dartmouth Street (page 28). Ten years later it was dramatically enlarged in gleaming white marble to extend some 250 feet along Commonwealth Avenue. In its prime it was among the most admired buildings in Boston, and in 1882 it became the city's first commercial building to install electric lights. A 1972 fire destroyed much of the original building, and renovations have altered its old Parisian roofline. Today the Vendome accommodates 27 business suites on the lower floors and 110 condominium apartments above.

Arches. In the shadow of the Vendome addition are two buildings from the same decade. Picturesque and characterful, they seem undaunted by their imposing neighbor. Number 172 is another work of J. H. Besarick. At the roofline are Romanesque arches trimmed with the architect's trademark foliate carvings. Two doors down at Numbers 176-178 is a wonderful building by Charles Atwood. Here the arches open onto the street, the three openings giving entry to two separate houses that are capped with dormers and towers and a fantastical curved gable.

A proper Bostonian. Back Bay's oldest surviving French flat, the Hotel Agassiz still commands its Exeter Street corner. It was erected in 1872 at the farthest reaches of the Back Bay lands and stood alone for most of the decade. The Agassiz was the venture of Henry Lee Higginson, one of the richest and most generous Bostonians of his day, who almost singlehandedly founded and funded the Boston Symphony Orchestra. Like its early residents, the building was a proper Bostonian, understated and dignified. It originally held six grand floor-through suites that were occupied by Higginson, his brother-in-law Alexander Agassiz, and four other families. Today the complex includes a neighboring town house and contains 15 condominium units.

Terracotta. At 63 Marlborough Street (page 47), J. Pickering Putnam had designed the district's most vibrant display of panel brickwork. Here at 195 Commonwealth Avenue he concocted another marvel in custom-made terracotta. English terracotta had first come to Boston in the 1876 Museum of Fine Arts (page 23), but when this house was built five years later, the material was available locally. The Boston Terracotta Company created these pieces, which had been molded by John Evans, the master stonecutter whose name is usually identified with Trinity Church. The house was designed for Dr. F. C. Haven with his physician's office in a first-floor suite.

The St. Botolph Club. During Back Bay's boom years, a few well-to-do residents bypassed local architects in favor of the celebrated New York firm of McKim, Mead and White. Most Boston work was overseen by Charles Follen McKim, who in 1890 designed this house at 199 Commonwealth Avenue for J. Arthur Beebe. The style is pure Federal revival, inspired by Boston's own architectural past; only the plate glass windows distinguish it from a Beacon Hill dwelling of 1800. For thirty years it has been home of the St. Botolph Club, founded in 1880 "to promote intercourse among authors and artists and other gentlemen." Historian Francis Parkman was its first president, and it became the most sophisticated club of if its kind in Boston. It mounted the first American show of John Singer Sargent's paintings in 1888, and also sponsored the first American showing of works by Monet.

The Algonquin Club. An 1887 design by McKim's partner Stanford White, 217 Commonwealth Avenue has the self-assured look of a New Yorker. It was commissioned by the Algonquin Club, founded in 1885 as a social organization that also provided "a place to do business in private." White created a Renaissance palazzo in granite and limestone, distinguished by a grand two-story colonnaded porch and elaborate carvings in high relief. Among Back Bay buildings, this is one of only a handful still belonging to the original owner and still serving its original purpose.

The Mason and Cochrane houses. In addition to their bowfronts and Federal spirit, these two houses are remarkable because both were owned by the original families well into the twentieth century. Above is Number 211, designed in 1883 by the well-known firm of Rotch and Tilden for financier William Powell Mason. It was the home of Mason's daughter Fanny until her death in 1950. Miss Mason was a friend and traveling companion of fellow-collector Isabella Stewart Gardner. Below is the 1886 Alexander Cochrane house at Number 257. Another design of McKim, Mead and White, the house stayed in the Cochrane family until the 1940s. Both buildings have especially fine and well-preserved interiors; the Mason House has been recycled into office space, while the Cochrane House contains six condominiums.

International Institute. Rotch and Tilden also designed the double-width dwelling at 287 Commonwealth. This refined composition in limestone dates from 1892. Its Classical spirit is announced by a columned Greek portico crowned with an anthemion crest, a motif that reappears at the roofline. When the house was just twelve years old, much of its interior was redesigned by Ogden Codman. Remaining in the Sears family until 1942, it now belongs to the International Institute, a social-service agency founded in 1924 to give support and assistance to foreign-born residents.

303 and 305 Commonwealth Avenue. A decade apart, these two relatively narrow houses offer a study in contrasts. The dwelling on the left was built in 1884, the work of architects Peabody and Stearns. Probably the most prestigious local firm, they were also enormously productive, credited with at least seventy Back Bay designs. Their brick-and-brownstone house at 305 Commonwealth is almost austere, except for the wonderful roof gable with a crocketed pinnacle rising from a lion's head. The house next door, Number 303, dates from 1895. Constructed of white granite, it is the last Back Bay house by McKim, Mead and White. The facade takes the form of a single broad bow with a central entrance, and decoration is limited to chaste Classical motifs.

Roses. One of the great delights of the modern neighborhood is the number and variety of front yard gardens. These pocket-sized plots are perfect for individual efforts, from trim evergreen hedges to virtuoso displays, like this rose garden at Number 240 Commonwealth Avenue.

"The Burrage." Today a retirement home, this turreted stone castle from 1899 bears the name of its builder, copper magnate Albert C. Burrage. The only Back Bay residence that aspired to the conspicuous grandeur of Fifth Avenue, it was designed by the Boston architect Charles E. Brigham. The style derives from the sixteenth-century Loire Valley, most particularly from the château of Chenonceaux, and although the flamboyant ornamental treatment may be ostentatious, the mansion displays superb materials and workmanship inside and out. Burrage, a self-made man, pursued hobbies in mineralogy and horticulture. From the Hereford Street side of his mansion, one can glimpse his orchid house with a curved glass roof and dome, now used as a sunroom by residents.

The Ames Mansion. The largest and costliest mansion of its day, the Oliver Ames house at 355 Commonwealth Avenue dates from 1882. Ames was president of the Union Pacific Railroad and governor of Massachusetts. His house, designed by Carl Fehmer, is an extravagant building, often overlooked because of its location (opposite the 1937 underpass at Massachusetts Avenue) and its somber massing in brownstone. But a closer look reveals remarkably delicate detailing, especially in the carved frieze that wraps around the house above the first-floor windows. It shows a procession of cavorting cherubs performing activities appropriate to the rooms behind the windows. Until recently the house has been occupied by Emerson College, which maintained the lavish interiors (page 106) as administrative offices.

Alexander Hamilton, 1865, by William Rimmer

General John Glover, 1875, by Martin Milmore

Leif Ericson, 1887, by Anne Whitney

William Lloyd Garrison, 1886, by Olin Levi Warner

COMMONWEALTH AVENUE MALL

The heart of the Back Bay residential district, Commonwealth Avenue Mall serves as promenade, playground, and site of varied neighborhood events. Its fortunes are monitored by a watchdog citizens group whose concerns include the health and maintenance of trees and the physical condition of fences, benches, and lawns.

The first piece of sculpture to arrive on the Mall was William Rimmer's Alexander Hamilton in 1865 (opposite), said to be the first granite statue in America. Like all the Mall's statuary, Hamilton faces east, toward his commander-in-chief General George Washington, whose equestrian statue looks down the Mall from the Public Garden. The later pieces were cast in bronze. Also seen here are memorials to John Glover of Marblehead, whose marine regiment transported Washington's army by water — including the famed Delaware crossing; the Norse hero Leif Ericson, commissioned with funds raised from the Norwegian-American community; and Boston's fiery abolitionist William Lloyd Garrison. All Mall statuary is included in the city's Adopt-a-Statue program, which secures endowments for preservation of public art.

NEWBURY STREET
Bon Ton

WITH ITS CHIC GALLERIES and stylish boutiques, Newbury Street numbers among the nation's choice shopping districts. It began, however, as a residential thoroughfare on the scale of Marlborough Street — which it resembles in early photos. But it never achieved the prestige of the "Three Streets" to the north, and by 1930 its eastern end was almost completely occupied by storefronts.

The original Museum of Fine Arts, which opened in Copley Square in 1876, served as a magnet for other art-related activities that spread northward to Newbury. The street soon became home to the Boston Art Club (page 86), Massachusetts Normal School (today's Massachusetts College of Art), and the St. Botolph Club, as well as numerous small galleries. This focus on art continues today. The upper end of the street is more lively if less chic, characterized by rows of houses built on speculation, their lower floors converted to shops. The final block was once devoted to stabling.

Perhaps Newbury is a more interesting street today than during its residential years. The long rows of nearly identical houses have been individualized by storefronts. The old bay windows lend themselves nicely to being display windows, and the twenty-foot setbacks have been effectively adapted for kiosks, sidewalk cafes, or open-air displays. From end to end the street exhibits a lively commercial air that attracts shoppers and browsers year round.

NOTED RESIDENTS:

Phillips Brooks, theologian, bishop 233 Clarendon

Charles E. Cummings, architect Number 109

J. Pickering Putnam, architect 277 Dartmouth

*Al fresco. Newbury Street's sidewalk cafes and
high-style shops lend a cosmopolitan atmosphere
that lures diverse weekend crowds of window
shoppers, gallery hoppers, and people watchers.*

The Ritz. Since opening its doors in 1927, Boston's Ritz-Carlton has catered to a dazzling array of world leaders and celebrities including Winston Churchill, Mikhail Baryshnikov, Katharine Hepburn, Presidents Kennedy and Johnson, Prince Charles, King Hussein, Lena Horne, Lassie, and Morris the Cat. Rogers and Hammerstein rewrote many a song here during the era of pre-Broadway tryouts; Rudolph Nureyev once danced on the bar at an after-hours soirée of the Royal Ballet troupe. The Ritz still imparts an air of glamor and romance, whether dining in elegance overlooking the Public Garden, relaxing at fireside in the mahogany-paneled bar, or dancing under the stars on the open-air roof.

Emmanuel Church. Emmanuel was the second church to be built in Back Bay and the earliest in the rural English Gothic style. Moreover, it was the first church of puddingstone, the local conglomerate admired for its rich, warm hues that became almost synonymous with Back Bay churches. The building one sees today is much altered from the original of 1862, which was smaller and freestanding, facing east onto a churchyard. In 1898 it was enlarged and the entrance moved to streetside. Finally, in 1920 the Leslie Lindsay Memorial Chapel was erected in memory of a young victim of the Lusitania tragedy. The chapel has a dramatic interior in the perpendicular Gothic style.

Trinity Rectory. Despite a radical roof-raising, this is essentially the house that H. H. Richardson designed for his friend Phillips Brooks in 1879. It was Brooks who moved Trinity Church to Back Bay in 1872 and served this parish for twenty-two years. He also wrote lyrics for the popular Christmas carol, "O Little Town of Bethlehem." When Brooks became Bishop of Massachusetts in 1891, his old bachelor's quarters proved inadequate for the family of the new rector, so they were enlarged by inserting a new third floor under the original roofline.

Architectural residences. Early Newbury Street was soon dominated by undistinguished spec houses, but the two buildings pictured here are exceptions. At opposite ends of the Clarendon/Dartmouth block, they have much in common. Both are commanding corner houses, medieval in inspiration. Moreover, both were built by architects as their own homes. On the left, Number 109 (1871) was the house of Charles E. Cummings, whose firm Cummings and Sears designed more than twenty Back Bay houses. Like his Old South Church, Cummings's residence is picturesque and elegant. The other house, 277 Dartmouth Street (1878), was the home of J. Pickering Putnam. Both buildings have been stylishly adapted as shops.

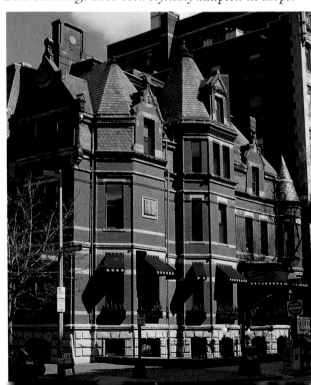

The Newbury Street Mural. Enlivening the streetscape, the Newbury Street Mural is "an architectural fantasy" painted on a five-story brick wall overlooking a parking lot. Crowded into the ground-level cafe are about sixty men and women, each with a local connection. Above are "visual quotations from the history of art," including figure by Michelangelo, Rembrandt, Copley, and Degas. The mural's design was derived from competition entries of local art students, and the painting was completed in 1991. A key to the figures is attached t the iron fence facing Newbury Street.

The Prince School building. For more than a century this imposing brick edifice served as a public grammar school for Back Bay children. In 1982 it was very successfully recycled, with ground-floor shops along Newbury Street and 36 condominium units above. The parking lot in the foreground was the site of the old Massachusetts Normal School (now Massachusetts College of Art); it is currently the focus of controversy over a proposed commercial development.

Newbury Street stables. The final block of Newbury Street, between Hereford Street and Massachusetts Avenue, was the only section of Back Bay never controlled by deed restrictions, and it was generally devoted to stabling. Many of the original buildings have survived, providing a pleasant contrast in scale and style with the rest of the district.   All these old stables have now been converted to commercial use, and the block has a cheerful, trendy character, a blend of prosperity and bohemianism.

Murals. On the same block are two other outdoor murals. On the left is the "Tramount Mural," a surrealistic painting on steel panels in front of a rapid transit facility. The work of Morgan Bulkeley, it dates from 1981. The graffiti is of more recent vintage; the Back Bay neighborhood has been in the forefront of efforts to enact strict anti-graffiti laws. On the right is a trompe l'oeil wall painting by Richard Haas, executed in 1977 on the western wall of the Boston Architectural Center. It presents a sectional view of a Renaissance dome with several human figures peering out across the skyline. The BAC, founded in 1889, offers a flexible degree program with many courses conducted by volunteer architects.

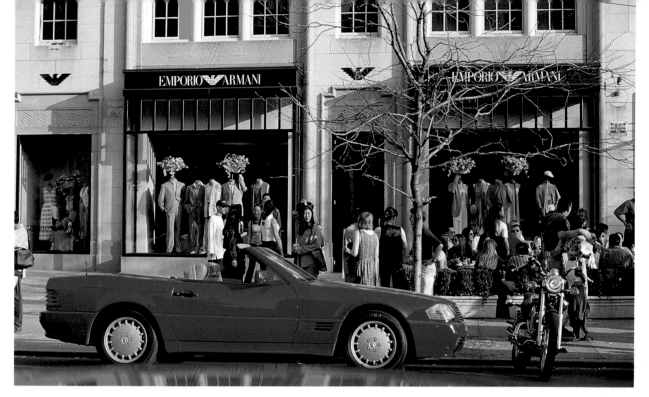

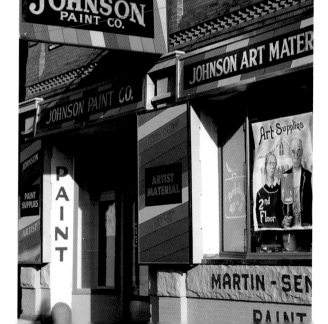

BOYLSTON STREET
Strictly Business

BOYLSTON STREET, like Beacon, is an extension of an older roadway. Indeed, this most cosmopolitan of Back Bay streets can trace its origins to the colonists' path along the southern edge of Boston Common, once called Frog Lane.

The bustling commercialism of the modern street belies the intent of Back Bay planners, who foresaw this southernmost avenue as a residential street of high fashion — only Commonwealth Avenue and Boylston Street banned commercial activities. This vision never took shape, and stores soon appeared along the lower end of the street. In 1898, the street was released from clauses forbidding commerce, and the last private residence disappeared in the 1920s. For several decades mid-Boylston had an air of Fifth Avenue, with local branches of several New York department stores; the last survivor of this era, Bonwit Teller, occupied the old Museum of Natural History building, seen on the opposite page.

Much of the street has lost its human scale as the town-house modules have been obliterated by megabuildings and commercial complexes. Each decade of the modern era has left a mark: In the 1960s the Prudential Center heralded the beginnings of the "New Boston"; the 1970s saw the development of Park Plaza along Back Bay's eastern boundary, and with the eighties came the works of the post-modernist architects Johnson and Stern. Finally, the expansion of the Prudential complex and the Hynes Convention Center in the 1990s forced modern Boylston Street farther westward.

Landmarks. In the foreground, the F. A. O. Schwarz bear commands the corner of Boylston and Berkeley streets. Beyond it is the 1863 Museum of Natural History, today a clothing store. This building once stood almost alone at the edge of the Back Bay flats (page 17), then as now a landmark.

Old favorites. Pictured above are two long-time Boylston Street emporiums, Shreve, Crump and Low, and the Women's Educational and Industrial Union. The Shreve building dates from 1904; when the jeweler arrived in 1930, the facade was given a contemporary art deco look. On the right, the golden swan marks the entrance to the Union's tasteful Boylston Street shop. The WEIU was founded in 1877 "to teach immigrant women millinery and culinary skills." Above the shop are classrooms and offices.

Confection. Recently restored, the 1905 Berkeley Building animates its busy Back Bay intersection. It is the design of Desiré Despredelle, a French architect who for twenty years taught design classes nearby at MIT's School of Architecture. The facade is composed of enameled terracotta and glass applied to a lightweight steel frame. Bostonians have always liked this building, which architecture critic Robert Campbell styled "a wedding cake of a building with white terracotta icing."

*Postmodernists. **T**wo buildings from the eighties bring postmodernism to Boylston Street. On the left is 222 Berkeley by Robert A. M. Stern with Jung Brannen; on the right, the "new" New England Life Building by Philip Johnson. The Johnson building was the focus of strong dissent. Its original design called for twin towers side by side, but following a lawsuit by neighbors, the second tower was redesigned by Stern and substantially reduced in height.*

Survivors. In the 700 block of Boylston Street is a rare surviving pocket of buildings that retain a nineteenth-century scale, a reminder of the street in the pre–World War II era. Erected in 1901, they have served at various times as an automobile club, a furniture warehouse, and a school for aspiring models. They are currently occupied by an assortment of retail stores and eateries.

COPLEY SQUARE

*"A grand basilica." So declared Boston newspapers
upon the 1877 consecration of H. H. Richardson's
Trinity Church. Modern-day critics tend to regard
Trinity as the architect's masterwork, the
quintessence of "Richardson Romanesque." The
weight of the great square tower, which dominates the
building inside and out, is supported by 4500 wooden
pilings. The porch, considerably more decorative
than the rest of the building, was added in 1897,
after Richardson's death. The interior, designed by
John La Farge, contains a wealth of stained glass,
mural paintings, mosaics, carved wood, and sculpted
stone. Against Trinity's northern wall (right) is a
monumental sculpture of Phillips Brooks, the rector
who helped create this building. Dedicated in 1907,
the memorial was the posthumous work of both the
sculptor, Augustus Saint-Gaudens, and Charles F.
McKim, who designed the architectural surround.
Looming 62 stories above Copley Square is the 1976
John Hancock tower, the controversial skyscraper by
Henry Cobb for I. M. Pei and Partners. Even the
building's detractors grant its elegance. Its thirteen
acres of glass walls create breathtaking images of its
famous neighbors with ever-changing skies. On a
clear day the view from the observatory extends a
hundred miles.*

"A palace for the people." These words shaped the vision of Charles F. McKim's Boston Public Library, which was begun in 1888 and opened seven years later. The first public building in America in pure Renaissance style, it was to Henry James "a Florentine palace magnificently superceding all others." Like a sculpted work of art, the building stands on its own platform overlooking Copley Square, its entry flanked by Bela Pratt's heroic sculptures of Art (below) and Science. Stone panels on the upper-level arcade bear the names of leading cultural figures of history. Inside is a splendid array of sculpture and paintings, and in the center a lovely cloistered courtyard. Though costs soared high over budget, the building was widely acclaimed, and a hundred years later McKim's people's palace still dazzles the eye.

The Copley Plaza. On the site of the original Museum of Fine Arts, the 1915 Copley Plaza Hotel has proud credentials, the work of Clarence A. Blackall, designer of movie palaces, and Henry Hardenberg, architect of New York's renowned Plaza Hotel. The stone lions guarding the entrance are older than the hotel itself and have a colorful history of their own. Dating from 1899, they were modeled from "Wallace," a popular attraction at the Boston Zoo. They once stood several blocks down Boylston Street, in front of a residential hotel named the Kensington. That structure was razed, and in 1967 the lions were grandly gilded and moved to Copley Square.

Old South Church. Following the dictums of British tastemaker John Ruskin, the "new" Old South Church of 1874 took inspiration from the Gothic churches of northern Italy. Picturesque and flamboyant, it was the design of Cummings and Sears. Its puddingstone walls were elegantly trimmed with polychromatic stonework, and its original 220-foot campanile (page 23) was an architectural wonder — until it began to tilt. Leaning increasingly towards the southwest, it was eventually 36 inches out of plumb and in danger of toppling. It was finally taken down in 1931 — to the delight of Boston's press, who produced a spate of "Leaning Tower" stories — and rebuilt a few years later.

The Pru and the Hynes. Symbolizing the "New Boston" of the 1960s, the Prudential Center was erected atop the Massachusetts Turnpike and several acres of old railroad yards. The central skyscraper, soon known as The Pru, was completed in 1964 as the tallest structure in New England — until it was bested (by 40 feet) by the Hancock Tower. Criticized as remote and isolated, the Prudential has recently added a new shopping mall (above) that more effectively relates the complex to Boylston Street. West of the mall is another updated building from the sixties, the John J. Hynes Civic Auditorium. An in-town convention center operated by an independent authority, the Hynes was handsomely rebuilt in the late 1980s.

Engine House #33 / ICA. This arresting pair of brownstone buildings was erected in the mid-1880s as neighborhood police and fire stations. Although the buildings are still related architecturally, their functions have diverged. On the right is the firehouse, still operating as Engine House #33. The police station, however, was vacated in 1974, then gutted and rebuilt with several levels of contemporary exhibition areas for the Institute of Contemporary Art.

Arlington Street Church. "After the manner of Wren with a steeple such as our forefathers loved" — so wrote architect Charles E. Cummings of Arthur Gilman's Arlington Street Church. It was dedicated in 1861, and as the first sizeable building in the district, it was in a sense a feasibility study for future large-scale construction on the filled land. This was the church of William Ellery Channing, known as the founder of Unitarianism in America. Behind the Georgian facade is an Italian interior, modeled, said Gilman, after a church in Genoa. The sanctuary contains fourteen Tiffany windows.

ALPHABETICALLY SPEAKING

AN ARCHITECTURAL TOUR

FROM A(RLINGTON) TO H(EREFORD)

The basic concept of the Back Bay plan called for five parallel avenues intersected by eight shorter cross streets. These streets were not all named at once, but there soon emerged a sequence of aristocratic/Anglophilic names arranged alphabetically, Arlington to Hereford, westward with the fill. The sequential nature of the filling process has left us a tangible record of the course of domestic architecture in the nineteenth century. As it marches westward, Back Bay presents a changing panorama of the styles and tastes of Victorian-era America.

Bainbridge Bunting identifies some thirteen different architectural styles that appeared in Back Bay after 1860. More simply, however, there were three, each roughly identified with a decade: the French Academic of the 1860s; several concurrent variations of "Victorian" during the seventies; and a gradual return to classical forms in the eighties.

Of course, this kind of categorization is far too simple. Stylistic changes occurred gradually, overlapping in years and with never a precise beginning or end. Moreover, a single house frequently incorporated a combination of styles within a single design. Nevertheless, the trends are strongly apparent, and they reverberate on nearby avenues. The following tour of the cross streets will focus on the architectural footprints left by each decade of Back Bay's development.

ARLINGTON STREET
(laid out in 1859)

Of all the cross streets, Arlington makes the clearest architectural statement. Indeed, the men who planned the district were also instrumental in the design of these earliest houses, and even today the street reflects their vision. It was

Mansard Block. Attributed to Arthur Gilman and Gridley J. Fox Bryant, the three houses at 1, 2, and 3 Arlington Street are intended to read as a single grand edifice, such as Arthur Gilman would have seen on his recent trip to Paris. The ensemble utilizes the pavilion scheme, with the end houses projecting slightly to frame the central unit. Each level has a different window treatment, crisp and academically correct, and the entire ensemble is topped with a stylish mansard roof.

their effort to create in Boston the academic style of architecture then being practiced on the Continent — setting a standard of dignity for the new district.

This sophisticated new style took the form of freestanding groups of buildings, each block giving the appearance of a single grand mansion while actually composed of several separate dwellings. The designs are severe and disciplined with an emphasis on symmetry, and the distinctive "architectonic" framing around windows and doors. The favored building material is stone, especially brownstone, which is also utilized for balustraded parapets and balconies as well as for fencing at street level. Another distinguishing feature is the mansard roof, a Parisian import that will dominate the Back Bay skyline throughout the sixties.

Framed window and stone fence

Mansard roof

"Absolutely perfect." So proclaimed Oliver Wendell Holmes about the 1866 Central Congregational Church, whose 236-foot spire rose as the tallest in the city. The design of New York architect Richard M. Upjohn, the church has subsequently changed both name and denomination. Today it is the Presbyterian Church of the Covenant. This is another Back Bay parish with a treasury of Tiffany glass, in this case some forty windows.

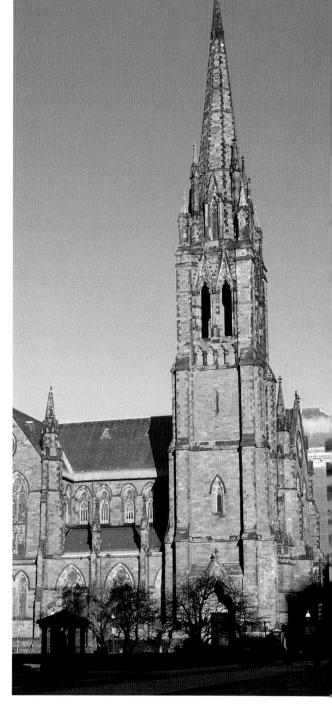

BERKELEY AND CLARENDON STREETS
(laid out in 1862 and 1870)

Berkeley and Clarendon were probably never completely successful as residential streets. Most corner houses were oriented toward the grander avenues, presenting long, uninviting walls to the side streets. As elsewhere in Back Bay, the corner lots were often occupied by churches and institutional buildings. Several are seen here.

Finally, these streets have suffered more demolition and replacement building than other cross streets. The few surviving residences, however, are strong reminders of the direction of Back Bay architecture around 1870, with a loosening of the rules of strict academic treatment. Flat surfaces give way to bay windows, and mansards are broken by towers and curving dormers. Red brick returns to fashion — now enlivened by a cautious introduction of contrasting colors and textures like panel brickwork, incised-line decoration, and the glazed tiles pictured below.

Panel brickwork

Glazed-tile insets

Incised-line decoration

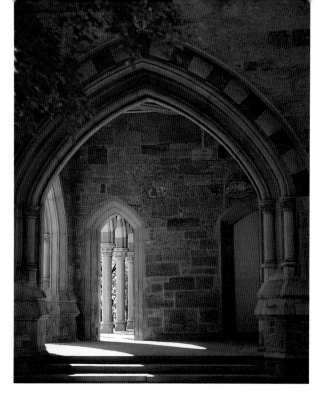

Reminders. A tall stone steeple and an arched carriage porch are all that remain of the English country Gothic church at the Berkeley-Marlborough corner, destroyed by fire in 1968. Designed by architects Ware and Van Brunt, it was completed in 1867 for the First Church, the original Puritan congregation in Boston. Following a 1970 merger, it became "The First and Second Church," now a Unitarian-Universalist parish, which commissioned Paul Rudolph to design a new building incorporating the few surviving remnants of the old. The statue of John Winthrop is by Richard S. Greenough.

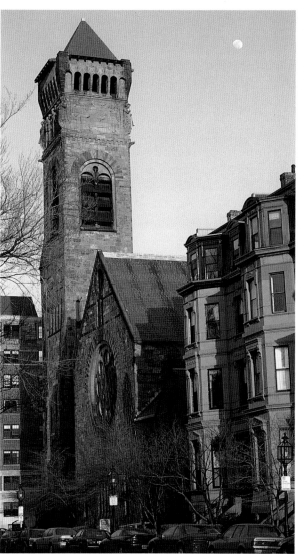

Important commission. Noted principally for its remarkable tower, the 1871 Brattle Square Church gave 31-year-old Henry Hobson Richardson his first important Boston commission. An acoustical disaster, the new building also bankrupted the Brattle Square congregation, which subsequently sold it to a Baptist parish. The tower frieze, depicting the sacraments of the church and trumpeting angels, was modeled by another young artist, Frédéric-Auguste Bartholdi, whose fame would rest on a later work, the 1886 Statue of Liberty.

Boston Art Club. Somewhat derelict, this Queen Anne charmer is the work of William Ralph Emerson, a local architect remembered mostly for his shingle-style country houses. It displays the sense of whimsy that marks many of Emerson's designs, with enormous cut-brick scrolls, an oversized fruit-bowl plaque (below), and an odd corner tower topped by a copper dome. The broad arch once opened onto the public gallery of the Boston Art Club. This group, founded in 1854, was one of a cluster of art-related activities that sprang up along Dartmouth and Newbury streets after the Museum of Fine Arts was established on Copley Square. Since 1970 the building has served as a public school.

DARTMOUTH STREET
(laid out in 1871)

Dartmouth Street was always envisioned as an important thoroughfare, a double-width street and a principle link with the South End. It was also a street of fashion, and some of Back Bay's finest structures still stand here, often freestanding on the Dartmouth Street side.

This is predominantly a street of the seventies and early eighties, an era of increasingly individualistic architecture. Brownstone is out of style, mansards are disappearing, and there is a continuing interest in ornamentation and a fascination with the "picturesque" — as evidenced by the rooflines seen here. A comparison of the houses on these pages with the austere Arlington Street blocks reveals the wane of the French-inspired academic style. In its place is a distinct echo from High Victorian London, with its potpourri of decorative devices and building materials — from the Ruskinian polychromy of Old South Church to the cut brick and terracotta of the early eighties. This was the golden age of cast-iron decoration, which enlivens the streetscape throughout the district. A particularly handsome example, the fencing at the Ames-Webster house, is seen at left.

Polychromatic stonework

Cast-iron fencing

Cut-brick plaque

In limbo. A delightful clutter of mansards and towers and dormers and mighty chimneys, the roofline of 315 Dartmouth Street sets a standard for Victorian extravagance. Dating from 1879, it was designed by Sturgis and Brigham, but its flamboyant roofline was added later (see Marlborough Street photo on page 30). One of the handsomest buildings in the district, the house served as a clinic for several decades; it is currently unoccupied, its future in limbo.

The Ames-Webster house. Bearing the names of the two families most closely associated with its history, the mansion at 306 Dartmouth Street remained in the Webster family into the 1960s. Its present design is by John H. Sturgis, who in 1882 enlarged and lavishly rehabilitated an earlier structure for railroad magnate Frederick L. Ames. Restored and recycled into office suites, the house still retains some of the most opulent rooms in Back Bay (pages 108 to 109).

The First Spiritualist Temple. Unrelated to the great architect except by the common name, the firm of Hartwell and Richardson shows a considerable stylistic debt to the Romanesque designs of H. H. Richardson. This 1884 church was erected as a center for the secular study of spiritualism. It has subsequently passed through several nonspiritual incarnations, first as a theater, then as a movie house, and today as a bookstore.

EXETER STREET
(laid out in 1873-1884)

In a sense, Exeter Street is architecturally out of sequence, presumably because it straddled the boundary between the land owned by the Commonwealth and that of the Boston Water-Power Company. In any case, the street was slow to develop and then received more than its share of large institutional structures — all four corners of Exeter and Newbury, for example, were once occupied by churches or schoolhouses. One of the survivors is pictured here.

In both public and private architecture, however, one encounters a new influence, neither French nor English but springing from Back Bay itself. H. H. Richardson's 1875 Trinity Church was hailed as a masterpiece, and its robust style soon reverberated across the nation. Here along Exeter Street are numerous Richardsonian features — rough-hewn stone facing, patterned stonework, deeply recessed porches, arched doors and windows — not only in institutional structures like the First Spiritualist Temple but in some of the larger residences erected in the early 1880s.

Patterned brick and stonework

Arched entryway

Queen Anne. Numbers 8, 10, and 12 Fairfield Street are an attractive ensemble, actually designed by two different architects. The corner dwelling, Number 12, is an 1879 work by Cabot and Chandler. Bainbridge Bunting points out that the ornamentation on this house includes no fewer than twenty different patterns of brickwork. The houses next door date from the same year. Designed by Sturgis and Brigham, they feature a common arched entryway and curved Dutch gables.

Terracotta plaque (above); pressed-brick work (below)

FAIRFIELD STREET
(laid out in 1871-1876)

Here is another cross street with a distinct architectural character. Fairfield Street offers a group of exceptionally picturesque buildings, the most notable cluster of Queen Anne-style houses in the district. The style originated in London, from which trends of fashion were being imported with remarkable speed by the late 1870s. Queen Anne buildings are characterized by color and animation: complicated, asymmetrical forms, rich detailing, and a new emphasis on high-quality workmanship and materials. Pressed-brick and terracotta work display greater variety, wrought iron returns to favor over factory-made cast iron, and the rooflines assume more romantic forms like the curving parapeted gables seen above.

Beginning here on Fairfield, the character of the Back Bay cross streets undergoes a perceptible change as many of the corner houses shift their orientation from the avenue onto the smaller street. The shift is extremely beneficial to these short blocks, which from Fairfield Street westward take on a more welcoming, domestic quality.

GLOUCESTER AND HEREFORD STREETS
(laid out in 1874-1880)

The Gilded Age never reached full flower in Boston, and with a few exceptions even the nouveaux riches seemed restrained by the city's basic conservatism. Nevertheless, the late 1880s and early 1890s produced Back Bay houses on a grander and more luxurious scale than ever before. In 1886, Charles Francis Adams, descendant of Puritans, built himself the imposing edifice at 20 Gloucester Street pictured opposite.

The dominant influence was probably the Beaux-Arts movement, with a return to a more disciplined, academic architecture. But now the focus had broadened to include architectural styles from a range of historical periods. The spirit of the age was captured by Boston's Paris-trained architect Robert S. Peabody when he declared: "Today this world of ours has pretty much agreed that so long as the work is artistic and excellent and appropriate, the historical style does not much matter."

Spurred by a period of unprecedented prosperity, this new architecture could be custom built to please the discriminating client. Thus one sees, side by side, dwellings inspired by Golden Age Athens, Renaissance Italy, sixteenth-century France, or Federal Beacon Hill, each a testament to the wealth and erudition of its owner. The New York firm of McKim, Mead and White produced a half-dozen Back Bay buildings, including the lavish John Andrew mansion pictured opposite. The cast-iron balcony overlooking Hereford Street (below) was brought from Paris, salvaged from the old Tuileries Palace. Another inspiration from Gotham was the Beaux-Arts splendor of upper Fifth Avenue, as echoed in the 1899 Burrage house (page 62) — and which ultimately derived from the castles of the Loire Valley. Another château-inspired motif along Hereford was the shell cornice, also seen below, at the Beacon Street corner.

All three houses pictured on the facing page were cited in the 1889 book *Illustrated Boston* as examples of particularly "costly and beautiful residences, in the erection of which architects have had no limit to the exercise of their talents, nor had their plans marred by lack of capital." The cost of the Adams residence was quoted at $80,000, the Andrew mansion at $100,000, and the Thayer house at $135,000.

Shell cornice

Palladian window and Tuileries balcony

Gargoyle

The John Andrew house, 32 Hereford Street; McKim, Mead and White, 1884

The Charles Francis Adams house, 20 Gloucester Street; Peabody and Stearns, 1886

The E. V. R. Thayer house, 17 Gloucester Street; Sturgis and Brigham, 1886

AN INTERIOR VIEW
Inside a Back Bay Town House

One [story] for eating, one for sleeping, a third for company, a fourth underground for the kitchen, and perhaps a fifth at top for the servants — and the agility, the ease, the quickness with which the individuals of the family run up and down and perch on the different stories give the idea of a cage with its sticks and birds.

— Louis Simond, 1817

The amused Frenchman who wrote these lines was reflecting on the domestic arrangements in a terraced house of Georgian London — the architectural prototype for the row houses of urban America. In Boston, these English-style city dwellings arrived early, most notably with Charles Bulfinch's 1794 Tontine Crescent, and reached full flower along the Greek Revival streets of Beacon Hill. The new South End was also a row-house district, and Back Bay would follow the same pattern. Moreover, Bostonians retained a lingering affection for their town houses, which they continued to erect despite the lures of suburbia. Completed soon after the turn of the century, the Back Bay district would be the last significant row-house development in the city.

In general terms, the interior arrangement of Back Bay's row houses did not differ significantly from those of Beacon Hill, or Tontine Crescent, or even Georgian London. The long, narrow lots that confined them allowed few variations from the "birdcage" model. Thus the drawings on these pages display the same upstairs-downstairs way of life that had fascinated Louis Simond.

What has changed, however, is the level of convenience and comfort within, and many recent technological advances can be seen in the ground floor of the house (see plan, opposite). Because the early district was prone to flooding, these rooms lie only a few feet below street level, and they are entirely functional, containing all the facilities needed for running an up-to-date Victorian household. A coal-burning furnace heats the house via a gravity hot-air system. A lavatory for servants signals the arrival of modern plumbing. In the front of the house is a laundry room with a stove and a built-in boiler tub. Like the rest of the house, the entire area was originally fitted with gas lighting, the standard method of illumination until the 1890s.

In the rear is the kitchen. The door to the brick-paved courtyard is actually the lifeline to the house, with all essential goods and services passing this way. The yard, in turn, leads to the service alley, a sixteen-foot passage paralleling the street. Today these byways give access to scattered garage spaces, but they were once scenes of bustling activity.

The kitchen itself is equipped with a built-in, coal-burning cooking range, which also heats the water for the house. (The ice box is kept outside the kitchen, in a cool wooden shed that occupies part of the yard.) Next to the kitchen is a small pantry with a dumbwaiter to transport prepared meals to the family dining room above; narrow service stairs also connect this area to the kitchen.

Despite all this modernity downstairs, the old way of life continued above, with the traditional vertical separation of social space. Our floor plans are based roughly on material prepared by Catherine L. Seiberling, former resident-guide at the Gibson House Museum. They depict an early Back Bay household of moderate but not unlimited means, and like Gibson House itself, they provide a strikingly authentic view of a working household in the Victorian era. As the years passed, Back Bay dwellings would become larger and more lavish, but in all except the grandest places, the basic scheme did not alter — one room in front and one room in back on each floor with a passageway and a staircase between.

On the first and second floors are the public rooms of the house, entered by guests and used for entertaining. Throughout this area, attention is given to a tasteful display of architectural ornament, particularly to woodwork and built-in furniture. Though the house is centrally heated, almost every room has a coal-burning fireplace not only to back up the furnace but for its symbolic and ornamental value as well. Carved hardwood or marble mantelpieces are often the focal point of public rooms.

On the second floor is the traditional double parlor, each room with its distinctive function and decor. The Gibson House front parlor is designated a library; with built-in bookcases, it probably served as an office for the man of the house. The back parlor, called the music room, was the realm of the ladies — for morning visits, afternoon teas, and evening entertainments.

Rooms above this level were reserved for the family and its servants. The third floor was a large master bedroom suite, consisting of two chambers, probably the separate rooms of the master and mistress, privately connected via a dressing room and bath. Finally, the chambers on the top two floors were the domain of female servants and family children, with sewing rooms, linen storage areas, playrooms, and nurseries.

But there came a time when most of these dwellings were deemed impractical. Dating from an era of large families and live-in servants, many were extravagant even in their day, and by 1950 the large town house was declared outmoded, its way of life extinct.

Miraculously, hundreds have survived, due in part to a timely recognition of their architectural appeal and value. Moreover, the very features that once spelled their decline were soon recognized as their greatest attributes. With ample size and vertical separation of space, the Back Bay town house has proved to be an exceedingly flexible piece of real estate — occasionally retained as a single-family residence, but more often adapted to changing times. The following pages provide glimpses into some of the houses in Back Bay today.

Ground Floor   *First Floor*   *Second Floor*   *Third Floor*

BACK BAY ORIGINALS
Victoriana

AUTHENTIC HIGH VICTORIAN interiors are surprisingly rare in Back Bay. Because the district remained fashionable, many of the older homes were eventually updated, frequently in a sophisticated Beaux-Arts manner. In more recent times, other buildings have suffered more cruelly through conversion into studio apartments or dormitories. On these pages are scenes from inside two early Beacon Street houses that were never changed. One, appropriately, is a museum, while the other is still a private residence. As a pair they provide a comparison between a relatively modest home of the 1860s and the residence of a prosperous merchant/builder.

Perhaps the greatest glory of these houses was their woodwork. Its somber richness, however, was often oppressive to later generations, who frequently covered the mahoganies and walnuts with layers of light-colored paint. In these two houses, however, the old woods have survived in their original splendor, only enhanced by the patina of living.

The prevailing tastes of the era were far removed from the chaste Greek Revival dwellings of Beacon Hill. Inspired by the traditions of the Renaissance, they displayed Italianate features such as round-headed arches and carved detailing with a heavy, sculptural effect. But the interior arrangement of rooms is not much changed from the Beacon Hill model, with an entry raised above street level; a long, straight staircase hugging the party wall; and a narrow passageway connecting the two main rooms on each floor.

A prosperous man's library, circa 1864, survives on Beacon Street. The richly paneled fireplace wall features an overmantel painting of Dante signed "A. Bicknell, 1866." This house has been in the same family for about eighty years.

*Seen here are views from two early Beacon Street houses, which share many features but also reveal the
differences between a relatively modest home and one of greater affluence. Above is the dining room in the
house of a well-to-do builder named Charles Freeland, with marquetry paneling, a built-in sideboard, and
oil-painted mahogany panels, set at eye level and commissioned especially for this room. Below, the dining
room in today's Gibson House Museum (page 38) retains its original sideboard, a freestanding piece
carved in black walnut, the wood that is used throughout the house. The table is set with green majolica.*

In the same two houses, the old-fashioned straight staircases resemble those of an earlier generation. The Freeland house (left) carries walnut wainscoting up the sweeping staircase — a lavish touch, like the carved newel post and elaborately turned balusters. On the right is the Gibson House stair hall, of similar proportions but with simpler balustrading and unpaneled walls covered with "Japanese leather," a heavy paper embossed to simulate hand-tooled leather. Below, a third-floor bedroom in the Gibson House holds a complete fifteen-piece bedroom set, circa 1870, crafted from bird's-eye maple to resemble bamboo.

BACK BAY DOMESTIC
Family Life in the City

DESPITE ITS HIGH-TONED public image, Back Bay was never exclusively the abode of the very rich. While great mansions were rising on Commonwealth Avenue, more modest dwellings were being constructed nearby. These smaller houses were concentrated along the western blocks of the district, especially on Marlborough Street, and as a group they have proved the most adaptable to changing times. Nicely scaled to modern living, many have been renovated by young families who have made the decision to live in the city.

The six houses featured on the following pages date from 1869 to 1881, thus bracketing the decade of the seventies. Much of this period was economically troubled, and the majority of new houses were relatively small. Their various histories reflect the changing fortunes that continued to affect the Back Bay neighborhood. A few have always been single-family dwellings, but more frequently they were taken over by institutions, or broken into small apartments or furnished rooms. By the 1970s, however, these houses were attracting the attention of a few families, who have restored, modernized, and individualized them. During the last several decades, the Back Bay family population has continued to grow, and today the district contains five nursery and elementary schools.

In a Marlborough Street kitchen, remodeled in 1988, the fireplace occupies the site of the old kitchen range. The bay, used as a family dining area, overlooks the walled garden seen on the following page.

Like all city back yards, this shady green garden was once a service area, providing a tradesmen's entrance to the rear of the house. Designed by the owner five years ago, it is lushly planted with a wide variety of material, including five specimen trees: Yoshino cherry, Carolina silverbell, Japanese snowbell, Japanese Stewartia, and European cutleaf birch.

This Beacon Street dining room was recently redecorated. The paneled walls have been papered with a colorful Oriental pattern, custom-made and hand-painted with peony and dogwood blossoms and butter-flies. On the sideboard is a piece from the owner's collection of whimsical ceramic tureens.

This pair of rooms emerged from a major restoration of an 1872 Marlborough Street house, once operated as a girls' school and then as a rooming house. Acquiring the building in 1982, the present owners salvaged a few original features, then set to work re-creating Victorian-era rooms. Collectors of antiques from all periods, they soon began to focus on Victoriana, especially paintings and sculpture. Gasoliers and period lighting fixtures have been added through the years, along with other appropriate pieces, such as the vast overmantel mirror in the parlor, which was purchased on impulse with the faith that it would fit perfectly — and it did.

Seen above is the library in a Marlborough Street house that has been in the same family for almost fifty years. It is a room of books and mementos, and its air of comfort is more accumulated than designed. This is the home of seasoned travelers, who have brought back objects from all over the world. Libraries became a common feature in Back Bay houses in the 1870s, reflecting the growth of the publishing industry and the increased availability of books.

In another Marlborough Street house, the original dining room is now used as a parlor. This striking red room features various special paint effects: a sponge and strié treatment on the walls, faux-bois framing for the mirror, and a marbleized mantelpiece. The antique Chinese carved elephant in the foreground is a souvenir of a recent trip to the Orient. The room also contains the owners' collections of early eighteenth-century Chinese Imari, and antique snuffboxes and card boxes.

On Beacon Street is an 1869 house that shows several layers of remodeling. The stair hall was updated in the early twentieth century in a somewhat Mediterranean spirit, with a Spanish tile floor, wrought-iron balustrading, and an airy, open feeling quite unlike that of the original tight passageway. The wainscot on the stairs is now painted, but it is probably original to the house.

Until ten years ago, this Fairfield Street house was broken into six small apartments. At that time it was rescued by a young family who retained one rental unit in the basement and returned the rest of the house to single-family use. Because most of the original detailing had disappeared, they could install modern conveniences with relative ease. Seen below is the living room, a nicely scaled room with a large bay window and a rare surviving element, the Gothic-style stone fireplace and overmantel of carved oak.

EXTRAVAGANZAS
The Spirit of the Gilded Age

FOLLOWING THE SLUGGISH 1870s, when Back Bay construction lagged, came an era of unprecedented prosperity as all across America new fortunes were made in industry and finance. Though Boston was now a mere provincial capital, it claimed its share of fortunes, which were frequently housed in new-found splendor in Back Bay mansions. The Ames family, for example, erected two grand residences in the district; scenes from both are presented here.

All these palatial dwellings are more or less identified with the movement known as Beaux-Arts. The style derives from the École des Beaux-Arts, the famed Paris institute that exercised increasing influence in America in the latter years of the nineteenth century. Its alumni became the leading practitioners of a sophisticated new architecture with an interest in historical themes and a new emphasis on interior decoration and planning. The Beaux-Arts architect was intimately involved with every aspect of interior design and to this end developed a coterie of artists and craftsmen to execute the elaborate detailing that was lavished upon the public areas of the house: stained glass, murals, ornamental plaster, fine woodwork and cabinetry — even entire suites of furniture.

Seen here are rooms from several mansions that exemplify the era. Large, lavish, and erudite, they reflect the Beaux-Arts spirit. Not surprisingly, none of them is a residence today, but none has been appreciably altered. As a group they illustrate a happy accommodation between modern use and architectural preservation. And though no longer furnished in the grand manner, these rooms still convey the sense of grandeur that made them remarkable in their day.

*This ballroom with French classical treatment
was added to Number 5 Commonwealth
Avenue around 1912, erected to accommodate
a daughter's debut. Today, both house and
ballroom are occupied by the Boston Center for
Adult Education, which rents this room for
parties and weddings.*

The earliest of the Back Bay châteaux, the 1882 Oliver Ames mansion was usually cited as the costliest and most sumptuous residence of its day. It was decorated by the celebrated New York firm of Herter Brothers, who were working on William H. Vanderbilt's Fifth Avenue mansion at the same time. Remaining in the Ames family until 1926, it was a casket company showroom for about fifty years, then became administrative offices for Emerson College. It is presently converted to commercial office space. As seen on this page, the interiors are still breathtaking. In the oak dining room (right), the paneled ceiling is supported by carved caryatids, figures from Greek mythology. Above the built-in sideboard, the original silk tapestry still covers the walls. A contemporary description identifies the style of this room as "early German Renaissance." Below is a corner of the former parlor, a grand salon in the continental tradition. In the cove of the gold-leafed ceiling, inset fire opals emit flashes of red light.

Members of the Burrage family lived in their 1899 mansion until 1948, but soon thereafter the house was converted to a clinic, its rooms sliced into offices and examination cubicles for physicians. Only the halls, stairs, and portions of the parlor and dining room were left intact. A multimillion-dollar restoration in the early 1990s refurbished the mansion as an assisted-living home for elderly residents. Above is a view of the restored parlor, a classical French salon. Below is the dining room, set for the midday meal for about thirty residents in an elegant hotel-style environment. Lavish and eclectic, the room is paneled in cherry and topped with a deep cove of gilded plaster decoration. The stained glass windows are a classical touch.

All the views on these pages are from the 1872 Ames-Webster mansion, which was enlarged and remodeled ten years later by architect John Sturgis. In its day this was undoubtedly the ultimate manifestation of urban luxury — though it was, in fact, outside the prevailing trend toward Beaux-Arts-inspired design. The scale throughout is magnificent, most notably the great living hall (opposite), glimpsed here from a landing on the monumental staircase. On this page are two views of the original music room, with its elaborately decorated ceiling and graceful boiserie. It now serves as a conference room and office for one of the building's several tenants. Below is the former musicians' gallery, now utilized for storage.

Measuring 18 by 63 feet, the great hall is the largest room in Back Bay. The grand stairway in the foreground had a ceremonial function: Guests would enter the house at street level, move by elevator to the second floor, then make a formal entry into the hall by descending these stairs.

From a corner of the mahogany-paneled dining room, the photo on the left looks into the conservatory, which faces south onto Commonwealth Avenue. Within recent memory this house was a private residence and the domed conservatory windows a Back Bay landmark, filled with seasonal floral displays from the owner's Brookline greenhouses. On the right is the original library, with embossed canvas-backed wall covering, probably the late-Victorian type known as Lincrusta Walton. This is the office of one of the principal tenants of the building, who was instrumental in its successful conversion to commercial use.

Above and on the opposite page are views from a Commonwealth Avenue mansion by McKim, Mead and White, which for forty years has magnificently housed an MIT fraternity. Designed in 1884 for John Andrew, congressman and son of a Massachusetts governor, the house contains some of the most distinguished interiors in Back Bay. Most of these rooms survive virtually intact, thanks to the Chi Phi fraternity, whose undergraduate members live here and conscientiously maintain the house. Seen above, an 1890 portrait of two little Andrew girls overlooks the paneled oval library in which they must once have played. A card lying on the mantelpiece identifies them as Cornelia Thayer Andrew, age 5, and Elizabeth, 3.

A hanging marble stairway with gold-plated balusters is the glory of this Beacon Street mansion, designed and decorated by the firm of Little and Browne in 1907. It has all the opulent features of the mature Beaux-Arts style; Little and Browne's account books reveal that $8000 was expended on lighting fixtures alone. An Adamesque delicacy is evident in every decorative detail of this house, which provides administrative offices for Fisher College.

In the Andrew House drawing room, an alabaster mantelpiece forms a stunning ensemble with an elaborate overmantel mirror featuring gilded wood fretwork. The painted ceiling rises from a sky-blue background to a scene of winged putti and garlands of roses. Below, the pine-paneled room on the ground floor was probably the congressman's office. Today it houses the Chi Phi pool table and a fleet of bicycles for the five-minute pedal across the Massachusetts Avenue Bridge to MIT.

BACK BAY CLASSICS
Life on a Grand Scale

THE DECADES BETWEEN 1880 and 1910 probably left the greatest mark on Back Bay interiors. Not only was new construction booming, but many older houses were revamped to reflect the more extravagant tastes of this extended period of prosperity. Whether originals or updates, these houses have several things in common: They are usually large — the lavish detailing requires a certain size to be effective — and they reflect the spirit of the Beaux-Arts tradition. Thus, interior decor tends to rely on architectural themes borrowed from the past, most typically from European sources or from Colonial and Federal America. Not uncommonly rooms within the same house display different styles, with a baronial entry hall, a Louis XVI music room, a Tudor-style oak dining room, and a Federal-period parlor — each magnificently appointed and historically true.

By this time the arrangement of rooms has become more flexible. An improved sewer system has eliminated the need for a raised entry, which now can be placed at street level with the kitchen moved to the basement. Thus one enters into a large, open entry hall in which the focal point is the stairway, which typically ascends via an impressive series of landings to an upper level of rooms.

The eight houses featured in this section are all owner-occupied; some are single-family residences, while others contain a rental unit or two. Not surprisingly, the owners usually retain the finest rooms of the house for their own use, with tenants using an elevator or servants' stairs to reach their quarters.

The house dates from 1872, but this spacious entry
hall was probably a later addition. The 1926
painting, entitled "The Muses," is by Frederick A.
Bosley, a prominent instructor at the School of the
Museum of Fine Arts.

This lofty room with its massive stone chimneypiece is probably the third incarnation for a second-story parlor overlooking Commonwealth Avenue. Built in 1861, the house was one of the earliest on the street. Its interior was drastically remodeled about twenty years later, when the entrance was lowered to ground level, and the dimensions of this room date from that time. However, the room seen here was probably created in the 1920s and reflects the current enthusiasm for vernacular Mediterranean styles.

Perhaps no architectural firm left a greater mark on Back Bay interiors than Little and Browne. Though they designed only three new houses in the district, they were responsible for the redecoration of dozens of others. Here are scenes from inside one of the firm's rare original dwellings, built on Marlborough Street in 1905 and occupied by its present owners since 1967. In the dining room, at right, an antique Waterford chandelier and a Turkish Oushak rug provide the finishing touches to a mahogany-paneled oval room. The round table was designed by the architects and has stood in this room since 1905. It expands to seat sixteen.

With a French mantelpiece, a large overmantel mirror, and paired classical sconces, this view of the drawing room exemplifies the refined delicacy and meticulous detailing of the early 1900s, when the Beaux-Arts style achieved its most elegant expression. The soft rosy colors of the Aubusson rug underscore the room's light and airy atmosphere.

Viewed from the stair landing, the second-floor reception area opens onto both dining room and drawing room. The inset oil canvases are probably French and were installed by the architects.

Around 1900, this early Commonwealth
Avenue house was extensively remodeled in a
classical European style. When the present
owner purchased the building in 1989, it had
been vacant for some time and was in poor
condition. However, the faded Beaux-Arts
interiors were so stunning that the owner
determined not only to retain them but to
redecorate and furnish the house in the same
spirit. The renovation has proceeded room by
room as a labor of love, and the photos on these
pages record some of the results. Above, a
breakfast nook occupies a skylit alcove that was
once a conservatory. The trelliswork and oil
panels date from that time. The mahogany
paneling in the foreground is part of the
original dining room, which now serves as
a library.

The dining room is furnished with nineteenth-
century revival pieces in the Sheraton and
Louis XVI styles. Overlooking the room is a
portrait of Edwina Mountbatten, the last
vicereine of India, painted in Paris in 1938.
The chandelier and sconces are French.

On the rooftop is a beautifully designed outdoor space offering views across much of the city. The applied motif on the built-in planters mimics that of the chair backs, and the deck is further defined by a low cast-iron fence. Scores of Back Bay houses have roof decks today.

A charming feature of this third-floor bedroom is an old mantelpiece painted to look like green marble — a common Beaux-Arts treatment for simple wooden mantels. However, this piece is actually made of stone, with Eastlake-period carvings discernible beneath its Beaux-Arts disguise. This delicately feminine room is bright and airy. The nineteenth-century silver tea cart is probably French.

The views on this page are from an 1872
speculator-built house that was grandly
refurbished around 1900 by Bigelow and
Wadsworth, a distinguished Boston firm. The
present owners have lived here for about fifteen
years. Their renovation has proceeded slowly, one
room at a time, so that each step of the process has
been carefully considered. Glimpsed through tall
paneled doors, the dining room (above left) is
fitted with an Elizabethan strapwork ceiling,
a silver chandelier, and a handsome parquet
floor. As elsewhere in the house, this room
retained many fine details but required
considerable restoration.

In the second-floor stair hall (above), a bay
window has a slightly exotic flavor, filled with
plants and various Oriental and western
antiques. The area also serves as a small,
semi-secluded study.

At left, the mahogany-paneled library is
furnished for comfort. The stone-faced mantel
is flanked by paired leather sofas, and the
sunflower arrangement picks up a favorite
Back Bay architectural theme.

H. H. Richardson designed this room in 1879 as a study for his friend, Trinity Church rector Phillips Brooks. Today it is the main living area for the present rector and his family. Above the mantel hangs a watercolor of the study during Brooks's residency. The room has not changed much, except for the white paint that now covers the finely carved black walnut woodwork — an "improvement" probably made in the 1920s. Like most parts of the house, this room is large but livable, attesting to the genius of its architect.

Brooks was a bachelor, but the present rector has a young family. This is a view of a third-floor bedroom, currently occupied by the rector's five-year-old son. A simple room, it was probably once used by servants. The window behind the bed provides a view of Trinity Church — preserved, it is said, when architect Ralph Adams Cram set back his 1939 New England Life Building to maintain a visual link between Richardson's church and his rectory.

Some of Back Bay's most beautifully restored rooms are seen in this 1880 Commonwealth Avenue house, which survived about fifty years of varied institutional uses until the present owners acquired the building in 1976. With only minor changes to the entry area, they were able to retain the integrity of this 26-room single-family house by creating their own triplex apartment including the skylighted grand stairway, and remodeling the upper floors as rental units. Removing temporary partitions, they found many original features undamaged. Restoration has been a continuing process, involving redecoration and finding appropriate furnishings for each room, including dozens of period fixtures installed throughout the house. Each room has a distinct character: The entrance hall (left) glows with the mellow tones of quarter-sawn golden oak. This view provides a startling contrast with the stair halls of earlier decades (page 97). Seen below, the library is now a home office. Its focal point is a superb mahogany wall, a rich display of cabinetwork with an array of shelves and cupboards, all built in to frame the fireplace. The beaded spindlework was typical of the period.

Oak, it seems, was the common wood of choice for paneled Back Bay dining rooms, and here the room is fully dressed in rich, somber tones. The furniture has been carefully selected to complement this effect. The thirteen matched Victorian chairs were acquired at three different stages from three different New England shops, and are especially prized because the floral motif carved on their top rail is similar to the design of the glazed tiles on the fireplace surround. The hand-painted floral-motif ceiling has never been restored.

In contrast to the russet tones of the other rooms, the white-painted drawing room is delicate in feeling, of the classical style typically favored for the family's most formal room. It has been furnished with an elegant simplicity using French, American, and English Victorian pieces. The Empire sofa and embroidered Chinese silk window hangings restate the classical theme.

Built in 1872, this Exeter Street dwelling was very nicely renovated in the late 1920s in a vernacular Mediterranean style, with stuccoed walls, arched doorways, and simple chimneypieces. Acquiring the house in 1978, the present owners appreciated many of these features, but as antiques collectors they also wanted some authentic period rooms. Accordingly, they have gradually returned parts of the house to its original appearance. For the living room, for example, they found a mantel of Eastlake design, roughly contemporary with this house. This room combines comfortable modern furniture with antique pieces. The Japanned tall clock to the right of the doorway was made in London circa 1750. In the adjoining dining room, they saved the silver chandelier and parquet floors, but re-created period woodwork and installed an eighteenth-century wooden mantelpiece salvaged from a house in Salem.

Always valued for their views, houses on the water side of Beacon Street were often designed to capture the vistas. In this 1881 residence, the rear room spans the entire 25-foot width of the house, with a projecting bay of tall windows rising to the 16-foot ceiling. With a mixture of classical and Baroque elements, the overall effect is grand. The owners, who occupy two floors of the house, bought the pool table for the family's entertainment; it also converts to a dinner table for large parties and holiday feasts.

The decorative scheme for this master bedroom began with the French linen fabric, from which everything else followed. The French theme predominates, with Nestle sconces, an Aubusson rug, and a bed, side tables, and chandelier all purchased from the same Paris apartment. However, the medallions on the mantelpiece are antique Wedgwood — considerably older than the house.

"HORIZONTAL LIVING"
From French Flat to Condo

THE CONTINENTAL NOTION of multi-unit residences came early to Back Bay, where the first French flat was erected in 1869. Others soon followed, and by 1890 there were about twenty of these family hotels with commodious suites of rooms arranged on a single floor (page 28). Based on Parisian models, the French flat offered the urbane Bostonian a maintenance-free home with a gracious suite for living and entertaining all on one level. This alternative was particularly attractive to people who had a country house and those who often traveled abroad.

There is a certain confusion between commercial and residential hotels — and indeed some establishments, like the Vendome, embraced both. Similarly, the distinction between apartment hotel and apartment house sometimes blurs, though the former apparently offered more amenities, such as an in-house dining room and maid service. In the course of the eighties, apartment houses slowly gained acceptance, and by the turn of the century they were established on every street in the district. A second wave of apartment-house construction dates from the 1920s and 1930s, and red-brick blocks from this era punctuate many corner sites. Well built and comfortable, they provide prime real estate today.

Boston's condominium craze of the 1980s began in Back Bay, which abounded in dwellings too large for a modern family, and in a sense the condo spelled the salvation of the residential neighborhood by creating hundreds of new owner-occupants. A fine old house could be sensitively converted into several units, each retaining some of the scale and decorative features that distinguished the original structure.

These pages feature examples of apartments from each era.

One of the most extraordinary rooms in the neighborhood, a Gilded Age music salon has become the master bedroom in a duplex condominium on Commonwealth Avenue. Each window bears the name of a composer.

This dramatic space is tucked beneath the sloping eaves of the old Prince School building. With large dormer windows and skylights above, this duplex condominium is bright and airy. Seen here is the view of the living area from the upstairs gallery, which leads to the master bedroom and bath.

One of the most interesting buildings in Back Bay is the Hotel Agassiz, erected in 1872 as six grand floor-through French flats. Through the years the original apartments were divided into smaller units, and there has been considerable moving of walls as the various units have changed in size, shape, and character. As a result, none of the fifteen condominiums in today's Agassiz are alike. Seen below is one of the smallest, a three-room apartment with the warm and comfortable feeling of a snug country cottage. The nineteenth-century French armoire provides valuable storage space, but the other furnishings are relatively small in scale, suiting the size of the rooms. This view looks into the candlelit dining room, where the Victorian chandelier has not been electrified.

On this page are two rooms from a ten-room penthouse apartment that is also in the Agassiz. The entrance hall (above) becomes an art gallery for the owner's own works and other contemporary pieces. Through the door on the left, Lucy stands guard over the artist's studio. At right, a large modern kitchen provides a comfortable eating alcove and a work area looking across Back Bay and the Charles River to the Cambridge shore.

When one of Back Bay's finest old mansions was broken into condominiums, the six main rooms of the house were protected as landmarks. Five of these rooms are within a single unit, which the owner has lovingly restored and redecorated with great respect for its historic value. Above is the library, with a 14-foot ceiling and superb walnut cabinetry. The mantelpiece is carved with roaring lions' heads, a patrician motif that appears elsewhere in the house.

The most unusual and admired part of this house is probably the dining room, installed by the China-trade merchant who built the mansion in 1871. All the major elements were fashioned of ebony in the Orient — the custom-carved sideboard, the woodwork, and a temple-shaped mantel with inset Ming plaques. The yellow porcelain lamp once burned whale oil. The decorated ceiling, which had long been painted over, was recently restored, revealing a delicate design of geometric patterns and flowers.

This exceptional condominium unit also includes the grand staircase, which is seen here ascending from the parlor floor to the bedroom area above. This view of the hall gives some sense of the grand proportions of the mansion.

Beyond the landmarked section of the house, the master bedroom is less formal, with various mementos of the owner's Texan origins: the Navajo blanket over the bed and the Lone Star banner alongside the bay window overlooking Dartmouth Street.

"It's a bit like living in the Sistine Chapel," admits the tenant of this extraordinary three-room apartment, all the more remarkable because it is a rental unit. The building dates from 1862, but these opulent interiors were installed in the late 1920s. Wrought-iron gates lend a Mediterranean flavor to the narrow stairway that rises steeply to the second-floor landing with a red marble fountain and spouting bronze fish. The gold-leafed walls are painted with romantic Italianesque landscapes.

This house had to be extensively rebuilt to accommodate fabulous installations like the vaulted ceiling and tall arched French doors overlooking Beacon Street. The gilded ceiling is inset with four oil-painted panels, and the room is dominated by a towering hooded stone chimneypiece. The unusual floor tiles are a Mediterranean azure blue in a pattern of alternating ovals and diamonds. This exotic room seems to be an ideal setting for the tenant's collection of Russian art.

A skylit stairwell and elevator landing has been fashioned into a conservatory.

Occupying the entire sixth floor of an 1892 Marlborough Street building, this seven-room apartment retains its original configuration. The scale is delightful, with two suites of rooms connected by a long, narrow hall. On the right is a small parlor in the reception area, furnished with art and antiques from three continents. An interplay of patterns and textures gives this room an exotic flavor — even the windows are hung with a heavy Oriental fabric. The owners are collectors and part-time dealers; before buying this apartment they favored American Federal period furniture, but in this setting their collection has gradually assumed a more cosmopolitan flavor. Above, the long central corridor has become a small art gallery.

In 1985, one of the most dramatic spaces in Back Bay disappeared when this two-story reception hall was divided between separate condominium apartments. Originally, the elliptical opening was surrounded by a balustraded gallery that looked down upon the ground-floor salon. Only recently was the area re-created when one couple acquired both apartments and re-opened the gallery in the ceiling. However, they have altered the space by installing a graceful flying staircase, which was prebuilt in Rhode Island and delivered to Commonwealth Avenue on six flatbed trucks. The 1886 mansion was designed by McKim, Mead and White.

In 1925, the developer of a new Commonwealth Avenue apartment building fitted out his own unit with a number of "extras," such as beamed ceilings, parquet floors, decorative ironwork, and a paneled dining room. The present owners of this nine-room apartment are a professional couple, who acquired it three years ago and undertook a complete redecoration. In the living room (above), the starting point was a 12-by-18-foot custom-made Chinese needlepoint rug, with vibrant colors that provided the palette for the room. The stuccoed walls were contemporized with a glazed and striéd effect; turquoise paint plays against the dark wood paneling in two adjoining rooms.

With its black marble floor and swinging iron gates, the foyer was given a more formal treatment. A classical pediment was added to the large gold-framed mirror, and prints of French garden plans were framed in gold with black reverse glass matting. In the niche is an Italian bronze reproduction of an antique piece. The needlepoint rug is Chinese.

RECYCLED
New Lives for Fine Old Houses

WHILE CONDOMINIUM CONVERSIONS were rescuing scores of large Back Bay dwellings in the 1980s, dozens of other houses had already been entrusted to institutional use. And indeed, this latter option has often proved the solution for a would-be white elephant.

Many institutional takeovers date from the post-World War II era, as old Back Bay families began to give up their city residences. Not uncommonly, a family would sign over its town house to a favored charity — Massachusetts General Hospital received 27 Commonwealth Avenue in 1942; Number 53 Marlborough Street was given to The French Library twenty years later. As other fine dwellings were offered for sale, many were acquired by schools and colleges already established in the district — Emerson, Fisher, and the New England School of Optometry all acquired spectacular properties at bargain prices in the 1950s and 1960s.

Larger Back Bay dwellings have proved suitable for all manner of group housing, from fraternities to residences for the elderly, while others have been converted into office facilities for both business and nonprofit groups. Whatever its nature, this kind of recycling raises practical issues. For the new owner, effective use of the building requires that some changes be made. For neighbors and preservationists, these gracious interiors are priceless legacies, irreplaceable and deserving of landmark status.

These pages spotlight rooms from some Back Bay houses that have been successfully recycled. An asset to the district and a tribute to their institutional owners, they can still shimmer as in their finest hours.

*What can be done with an old music room? While
the one on page 125 became a spectacular boudoir,
others have been converted into conference rooms.
The magnificent salon pictured here was added
to a Commonwealth Avenue mansion in 1897;
it now serves nicely as a meeting space for the law
firm that has restored the building.*

Like the music room on the previous page, these two rooms have been handsomely restored by a law firm, which acquired the 1883 mansion in 1974 and has preserved most of the building while at the same time using it for offices. For their own use, the two senior partners chose the original library (left) and the oval front parlor (below). As a pair, these rooms show how an architect of the 1880s gave different decorative treatments to the public rooms of a house. The library, with a quarter-oak coved ceiling, has been carefully appointed to enhance its rich and tawny elegance. In contrast is the parlor, with a light, classical air and delicate plaster motifs on the ceiling and the deep frieze that encircles the room.

Another fine Commonwealth Avenue residence is now occupied by the Commonwealth School. This house was designed in 1876 by architect Robert Gould Shaw as his own home, and the room seen here was once the dining room. The central stained-glass window bears a coat of arms, and the sideboard and mantelpiece are oak carved with the traditional dining-room motifs of fruits and trophies. The room is now the office of the head of the school, a coeducational day school that offers a college preparatory course for about 130 students.

Here is an early Commonwealth Avenue dwelling that was remodeled and redecorated by Back Bay's favorite Beaux-Arts architects, Little and Browne. This 1912 facelift created a second-floor parlor with the delicate detailing of a classical Parisian salon: a paneled and gilded ceiling, an eighteenth-century-revival mantel with gilt bronze mounts, and a pair of facing mirrors that multiply the shimmering reflections of the crystal chandelier. The house is now occupied by the Boston University Women's Council, which uses this room for meetings and receptions, and provides housing for sixteen graduate students on the upper floors.

Computers and file cabinets now occupy a first-floor room in an 1861 Commonwealth Avenue house that has belonged to Massachusetts General Hospital for some fifty years. Probably designed as an office for the original owner of the house, it remains an office today with all its ebonized cabinetwork still in place. The woodwork and built-in furniture display Eastlake-inspired decoration picked out in gold, and the ceiling has the heavy plaster cornice of the day. This room serves as the administrative office for Halcyon Place, which provides a home away from home for the immediate families of hospital patients.

This austere view gives only a hint of the time and money that were lavished on this Beacon Street residence before it was completed in 1900. Designed by Ogden Codman, its detailing was modeled on the great palaces of Europe, and its rooms contained architectural elements removed from houses in London and Paris. Italian workmen were also imported to execute elaborate plaster ceilings and cornices, like those seen below in the first-floor drawing room. This and an adjoining room are now combined as a lecture and conference hall for Goethe-Institut Boston, a German cultural foundation and language institute.

The Marlborough Street parlor of Henry and "Clover" Adams is now a sitting room at Hale House, a retirement home that combines the former Adams house and several connected buildings. On the main floor is an elegant suite of public rooms that include the splendid oval parlor seen here. Like the facade of the house (page 48), this room is old-fashioned and conservative, its oval shape and painted woodwork recalling Boston's Federal traditions. The sliding mahogany doors could be drawn closed for intimacy, or they could be thrown open to create a single large room.

This is a scene from the Kingsley Montessori School, which occupies an 1885 Fairfield Street house overlooking Commonwealth Avenue. The three-to-six-year-old class uses the original dining room of the house, much altered but retaining a few reminders of former times. Above the turtle aquarium is an inset oil painting that once surmounted a built-in sideboard. The school accommodates about 140 children between the ages of three and twelve.

A Back Bay kitchen, then . . .   *. . . and now.*

A Back Bay bathroom, then . . .   *. . . and now.*

The butler's pantry was once a vital part of the house, and virtually every Back Bay house had one. This was the place to which food prepared in the kitchen (usually located a floor below) was transported so the upstairs staff could serve the family in the adjacent dining room. The typical butler's pantry was equipped with a dumbwaiter, a small sink, and built-in cabinets for serving dishes; the view above is from the Gibson House Museum. With changing lifestyles, butler's pantries came to be seen as unused space, and relatively few of them have survived. Some were converted to closets or bathrooms, but more often they became kitchens, as seen below in a Marlborough Street residence.

142   BACK BAY

PICTURE CREDITS

We wish to thank the following institutions and individuals for graciously allowing us to reprint illustrations from their collections.

Abbreviations: **BA**, The Boston Athenaeum; **BPL**, Boston Pictorial Archive, Boston Public Library; **FPG**, Friends of the Public Garden; **MHS**, Massachusetts Historical Society; **SPNEA**, Society for the Preservation of New England Antiquities; **TBS**, The Bostonian Society/Old State House.

Page   Illustration

9   Trains crossing the Back Bay in 1844; engraving after drawing by J. W. Barber — Courtesy of Margaret Pokorny.

10   Western Avenue (now Beacon Street), as sketched by Lieutenant Colonel George Edward Head in 1847 — MHS. Beacon Hill and the Mill Dam, 1860; watercolor by N. Vautin — TBS.

11   Looking west from the State House, 1858 — BA.

12   Plan of a series of dwelling houses designed and erected in 1857 and 1858 by architect Nathaniel J. Bradlee; graphite and wash drawing — BA.

13   The Hot House in the Boston Public Garden, 1857 — FPG. The Meacham plan, as published in the *Boston Saturday Evening Gazette*, November 12, 1859 — FPG.

14   Proposed development of the Back Bay, 1824; photo reproduction of an aquatint by Abel Bowen — BA. General plan for enlarging and improving the city of Boston, Robert F. Gourlay, 1844; W. C. Sharp's Lithographic Firm — BA. David Sears's plan for Back Bay development, 1849; lithograph by Tappan and Bradford — BA.

15   Plan of the Back Bay lands, *Boston Saturday Evening Gazette*, supplement to the issue of April 24, 1858 — BA. Westbourne Terrace, Hyde Park, London, circa 1855 — Museum of London.

16   Beacon Hill monument; 1858 lithograph after a drawing of 1811 by J. R. Smith — BA. John Souther's shovel loading gravel for the Back Bay, circa 1860; photograph — BA.

17   Arlington Street Church, 1862; photograph, A. H. Rickards Collection — BA. Boston Society of Natural History, circa 1864; photograph by Josiah Johnson Hawes — BA. View of the Charles River Basin looking toward Beacon Hill and showing undeveloped blocks of Beacon Street, 1863–1869; photograph — BA.

18   Massachusetts Institute of Technology; photograph, A. H. Rickards Collection — BA.

19   Photographer on Commonwealth Avenue — SPNEA.

20   Henry Hobson Richardson, 1884; photograph by Marion Hooper Adams — MHS.

21   Hollis Street Church, late nineteenth century; photograph — BPL. Massachusetts Bicycle Club — SPNEA.

22   Peace Jubilee Coliseum, 1869; photograph, A. H. Rickards Collection — BA.

23   The New Old South Church, late 1870s; stereoscopic photograph showing the original campanile — TBS. Museum of Fine Arts; heliotype — *Winsor's Memorial History of Boston*, volume IV. Chauncey Hall School and Second Church, Copley Square (detail) — SPNEA.

24   Trinity Church — MHS. Boston Public Library — MHS.

25   Frederic MacMonnies's *Bacchante* at the Boston Public Library, November 28, 1896 — TBS. Copley Square from the roof of the Public Library, 1902; photograph by Baldwin Coolidge — BA. Boston Bicycle Club in front of Trinity Church, 1878; photograph — BA.

26   House of Albert C. Burrage, Commonwealth Avenue and Hereford Street; *American Architect and Building News*, November 16, 1901 — BA. Houses on Beacon Street for F. L. Higginson and C. A. Whittier; *American Architect and Building News*, November 24, 1883 — BA.

27   Residences of Mrs. D. N. Spooner and J. A. Burnham, before 1899; photograph by F. M. Smith (detail); from *Commonwealth Avenue and Its Residences* — BPL. Sleigh on Arlington Street at Commonwealth Avenue Mall — MHS. Horse car on Marlborough Street — SPNEA. Boys and girls exercising in front of the Prince School, 1893; photograph, probably by A. H. Folson — BPL. Commonwealth Avenue near Clarendon; photograph (detail) — BPL. 212 Commonwealth Avenue; photograph by Soule and Company (detail) — SPNEA.

28   Hotel Vendome, 1875; photograph — BA.

29   Drawing room of the Oliver Ames house, circa 1895; photograph — TBS. Dinner party at the Gardner home, 152 Beacon Street, 1891; photograph by James Notman — Isabella Stewart Gardner Museum Archives. Oliver Wendell Holmes, Sr., in his study, 296 Beacon Street; photograph — BA. Charles Hammond Gibson and John P. Marquand at 137 Beacon Street — *Life Magazine*, March 24, 1941.

30   Commonwealth Avenue Mall with Alexander Hamilton statue, 1880s; photograph (detail) — BPL. Marlborough Street, circa 1870 — SPNEA.

31   New Boston and Charles River Bay as proposed by Charles Davenport, 1885; lithograph by J. H. Bufford's Sons — BPL. Flooding back of Beacon Street, November 1898 — BA. The Esplanade, 1911 — TBS.

32   First Church in Boston; photograph by J. C. Hansen — BA. First Church in Boston, destroyed by fire, March 22, 1968 — BA.

33   Boston Public Library courtyard; photograph — Courtesy of Sara Cowles Walden. Mayfest, Halloween, and Alley Rally; photographs — Courtesy of Anne Swanson. Fishing on the Esplanade Lagoon; photograph — Courtesy of Barbara W. Moore.

34   Aerial photograph by Landslides.

All contemporary exteriors were photographed by Barbara W. Moore, and all interiors by Southie Burgin, unless otherwise noted. Maps and drawings on pages 8, 9, 12, 22, 28, 34, and 93 are by Constance Schnitger.